ADVENTURES OF A MISSIONARY NURSE

Tadpoles in the Milk

To Romelle's friend Terry:
May the Lord bless you.

Millie Gackle

MILDRED ROSEMAN GACKLE

Wasteland Press

www.wastelandpress.net
Shelbyville, KY USA

Tadpoles in the Milk
Adventures of a Missionary Nurse
by Mildred Roseman Gackle

First Printing – November 2018
ISBN: 978-1-68111-268-8
Library of Congress Control Number: 2018912651

Printed in the U.S.A.

0 1 2 3 4 5 6

This book is dedicated to my three grandchildren: Kaiah, Mason and Jakob Gackle. I wrote this book primarily for you because I want you to know more about what life was like on a mission field in the 1950s. May you each continue to follow the Lord and serve Him wherever life takes you.

ACKNOWLEDGEMENTS

Many hands and minds have contributed to the production of this book, and I am grateful for each one who helped.

I am extremely grateful to Ann Staatz for encouraging me to write about some of my experiences in Africa. Week by week she edited my stories, deleting parts or encouraging me to expand on a thought or an experience.

My thanks, also, to the members of the Homewoods on the Willamette Writing Club who listened to my stories with genuine interest in Africa, asked questions and made helpful comments.

Next, I wish to express my appreciation to Robin Schneider for typing my manuscript so it was easier to read, and for making the editorial changes week by week, each time the writing club reread a chapter. I thank her for her encouragement. She repeatedly told me she liked doing the typing because she liked my stories.

I am grateful to three pastors, all well-versed in missionary activity, who read one or more chapters and made helpful suggestions. My humble thanks to Don Hohensee, Bill Vermillion and Patrick Marunga.

My appreciation also to my son, David, and daughter-in-law, Vikki, who at my request, researched and made decisions about printing the book. Vikki also helped prepare the pictures for printing.

And last, I thank my daughter, Tricia, and her husband, Kerm Breakfield, who read the completed manuscript and made suggestions from the standpoint of those reading the material for the first time. They noted areas that needed further clarification, and statements that should be deleted.

TABLE OF CONTENTS

Charcoal drawing of a Kipsigis hut done by the author.

CHAPTER ONE
First Impressions

In August of 1950, at the age of 25, I traveled to Kenya, East Africa. Leaving home was hard; I did not know if I would see my parents again this side of heaven. But I was excited to be a missionary nurse for World Gospel Mission, a faith missionary society with work in the Highlands of Kenya.

As I was growing up, I had done little traveling; so a trip halfway around the world by train, steamship and airplane was a unique experience. I saw bits and pieces of places such as Chicago, New York, Liverpool, London, Southampton, Alexandria, Khartoum and Nairobi. From Chicago on I traveled with another first-time missionary, Louisa Ammerman. She was a school teacher going to Barundi and had a sister, Lillie Mae, who was a teacher at Tenwek, the mission station in Kenya where I was to be working.

From England to Kenya we traveled by "flying boat," a plane that landed on and took off from a body of water. In Southampton we took off from the Atlantic Ocean; in Alexandria from the Nile River; in Khartoum also from the Nile; and near Nairobi we landed on Lake Naivasha, a picturesque little lake surrounded by flat-topped thorn trees.

Even from high in the air, some of the trees appeared to be flat on top, and when I got on the ground and saw them up close, those flat-topped thorn trees immediately became one of my favorite trees.

When we arrived in Kenya, we found that Louisa's sister had had emergency surgery and was in the hospital in Nairobi. So Louisa's plans changed, and she stayed in Nairobi until her sister was ready to return to Tenwek.

In the 1950s, Kenya was an English Colony known as Kenya Colony, British East Africa. The Kenyan government was a colonial government with positions of authority filled by men from England. Immigrants had come to Kenya from other parts of the Commonwealth, making Kenya a land of mixed cultures. Three distinct cultures were obvious: African, Asian and European. The Asian group mainly was made up of Indians from India but included immigrants from other Asian countries. Americans were classed with the Europeans because of their similar ancestry.

Loren and Lois Clark, a couple I had known in college and also served with World Gospel Mission in Kenya, had come to Nairobi to pick Louisa and me up. I had to register with the government before going on to Tenwek. Lois took me to the right office and stood by while I gave the clerk the necessary information: my name, occupation, place of residence in Kenya, and family in the States to be contacted in case of an emergency.

During that short interview, I had my first culture shock. I had just told the clerk I was an RN, and he looked confused. Lois quickly spoke up and told him that I was a "sister." Now I was confused, and Lois explained to me, "They call nurses 'sisters' here." I soon found out that in English circles, RN means Royal Navy!

I was to be working with the Kipsigis tribe. Their tribal area was located about 250 miles northwest of Nairobi in the highlands near the big tea estates. We drove to Kericho, a small town on the edge of Kipsigis territory. The town had a hotel, a tea-packing establishment, a school, a hospital, a police station and numerous small Asian shops. From Kericho we traveled another 50 miles east by a secondary road to reach Tenwek (part of it a graveled road). That road was sometimes hard to travel during the rainy seasons.

Our tribal neighbors to the south were the Masai. If you have ever seen a TV documentary about Kenya, it probably featured the Masai. They were colorful and fiercely independent; had no desire to change; grazed large herds of cattle (30-50) in a game reserve complete with lions, leopards, cheetahs and hyenas; and considered bravery the most important characteristic of manhood.

According to Kipsigis oral history, when the Kipsigis saw the fertile area and the nice climate of the highlands, they drove the Masai out of the highlands and down to the plains, and the Kipsigis took over what had once been Masai territory.

The Kipsigis and Masai were traditional enemies. The government had attempted to ban tribal fighting. But periodic skirmishes still occurred along the border between the territories of these two tribes. (Might as well tell a lion to stop hunting antelope!)

From the western end of Kipsigis territory at certain points near Kericho, if you looked carefully, you could see the shimmering waters of Lake Victoria. Our tribal neighbors there were the Luo, and that is of interest because that is the tribe of President Barak Obama's ancestors.

Richard Adkins, a missionary who grew up at Tenwek and spoke and heard the Kipsigis language like a true tribesman, once took some of the elders on a hunting trip. Around the campfire in the evenings, he asked them to recite their oral history, and as they reached the end, it verified what some of the missionaries had heard from other sources: that the Kipsigis had been slaves in Egypt at the same time the Hebrew people were enslaved there. They had all been led out of Egypt by a hero named Musa, and years earlier they had gotten off a big boat that had run aground on the "Tulwet ab Araran." That would be Mt. Ararat to us.

Exodus 12:38 tells that other people left Egypt along with the Hebrews. None of these people are identified in any way, but according to their tribal oral history, the Kipsigis were part of that group.

Apparently the Kipsigis stayed with the Hebrews during part of the giving of the law. Some of the law of Moses appears in the Kipsigis culture:

1) They believe in One Great God
2) They have an annual Day of Atonement
3) They eat no pork
4) If a man dies young, one of his brothers is to marry the widow and/or care for her and her children.

Needless to say, I was experiencing much anticipation as we neared Tenwek Station. I knew I would be living in the single ladies' house – also known as Freedom Hall. I had only the 2 suitcases I had brought on the plane. My barrels of belongings and supplies would be coming later. My first assignment was to learn the language. Trudie Shyrock, the senior nurse, and Zakayo, one of the African pastors, were to be my teachers. Zakayo had served in the Kenya military and had at least one tour of duty in Malaya.

Tenwek Station was beautiful. It was about 15 acres on an eastern slope in the Kenyan Highlands. It had been terraced in several places to provide flat areas for buildings. At the top of the slope (6,800 feet above sea level) was the secondary school. Below that was the hospital.

A gravel road separated the school and the hospital and then circled down the south side of the property to the shop and the parking area. The hospital was comprised of about ten buildings and several open grassy areas. Some of the buildings were small but several were quite large. Most were made of cement blocks with concrete floors, but the OB ward was an old rectangular, mud-and-wattle building with a dirt floor and grass roof.

The beds in the OB ward had been made at Tenwek. They were wood frames standing about 2 ½ feet high. Criss-crossed ropes provided support, and ticks stuffed with dry grass and/or dried corn leaves and husks provided a degree of comfort for the patient. Because the women were used to doing things on the floor or ground, we at times would see a young Kipsigis mother standing on the bed, bending at her hips and reaching down by her feet to care for her baby.

The next three terraces down from the hospital were missionary housing. Freedom Hall was the first house on the south side and nearest the parking area. Below were the missionaries' vegetable gardens, and then on the right as one looked down the hill was a boarding school for African girls, and to the left a primary school landscaped with bright red canna lilies. And at the bottom of the slope above the river stood Hotchkiss Memorial Church. It had 3 large wings with many window openings. The sanctuary was furnished with simple benches – no back rests.

I can't remember that I ever walked behind the church and viewed the river from that point. But I often walked down to Tenwek Falls, a short distance to the left of the church. At the falls, on our side of the river, was a grist mill. One of the early missionaries had installed it. Now a local family owned it. Before the installation of the mill, the Kipsigis women had to grind their grain by hand between two stones.

During the dry season, we could walk across the river on the rocks at the top of the falls. Every season, the falls were great for taking pictures.

The climate at Tenwek was almost year-round nice. Kenya has no season changes as we do in more temperate climates. Tenwek had two dry seasons and two wet seasons. The sun was always potent, and we wore pith helmets to protect our brains and eyes and to prevent severe headaches. If you were too warm in the sun, all you needed to do was step into some shade. Even partial shade or filtered shade was 10-15 degrees cooler than in the sun.

Wearing heavy felt fabric protected from the sun too, so when I was home on furlough, I bought some heavy white felt and made an Emanual nurse's cap to take back with me. I earned the right to wear the Emanual Hospital cap because that is where I trained. I liked that much better than the helmet. When one of the Missionary Kids

(MKs) saw me wearing that cap for the first time, he said, "Hey, Auntie Millie, you look like an American nurse!"

A huge poinsettia bush grew in the residential area. Because we were south of the equator, the poinsettia bloomed from May to August. Another picture opportunity!

The Kipsigis people we served do not live in villages. They live on small farms scattered over the hillsides. The cattle and flocks have open-range grazing, but the people, usually the children, carefully herd the animals to keep them out of the gardens and to keep them from eating the thatch off the houses.

Kipisigis huts are round mud-and-wattle buildings and are fairly easy to make. The man starts the hut by firmly embedding long posts into the soil in a circular pattern. Then the family weaves small branches between those posts and fills in the empty spaces with sod and mud until they have a solid, even wall about 4-5 inches thick. They form the roof by tying a dozen or so poles together at one end and letting the other ends extend over the top of the wall at regular intervals. Then they cover those rafters with a thick layer of thatching grass, enough to keep a heavy rain from dripping on the floor below. Last, inside and out, they plaster the wall with a thin mixture of cow manure. This plaster dries to a hard, odorless finish that does not crack and therefore will allow no insects to hide in the walls.

The hut has no windows, and the door, which they "close" by a cowhide, is only about 4 feet high. The small door is for the protection of the people living inside. If an enemy comes, he must put himself in a most vulnerable position to bend over and walk through that door. And, because he has come from the bright sunlight, he cannot see a thing when he first enters.

In the center of the hut the family creates a small stone-rimmed depression for the fire. That keeps the home cozy and provides a place to cook food.

Across from the door along the wall, the builder constructs a raised earthen bed complete with raised earthen headrests at the head of the bed. Infants and small children often sleep with their parents on the bed, but when it gets too crowded, the older children will sleep on a cowhide on the floor.

Of course the floor is dirt, easily swept clean by a leafy branch available from almost any tree or bush.

In earlier years, the Kipsigis grew a millet they called "bek." Then someone introduced field corn. They liked that better because they usually got a much bigger harvest – and some of them liked the taste of corn better. Still, for special occasions, they sometimes made their "gimyet" from bek rather than corn. Like buckwheat, bek cooks up looking like chocolate pudding. The women cook their gimyet (a thick mush) in a clay pot over the small open fire in the center of the hut. The woman starts with boiling water to which she adds a handful of corn meal or bek meal. Then she uses her beater to keep the gimyet from getting lumpy. She gets her "beater" from one of the local bushes – the beater is a small branch that has 3 smaller branches growing out of the end. It looked similar to a chicken's foot. The woman cuts off the main branch below the three little branches and shortens the three little branches to fit her pot. She holds the main branch between her palms and rubs it briskly as she submerges the three smaller branches into the boiling grain. The little spinning branches break up any lumps and keep the gimyet smooth. She continues adding meal and using her beater until the product is thick enough to be broken apart and eaten like bread. I believe these women are talented far beyond us!

They tell me that a Kipsigis girl learning to make gimyet will break several clay pots before she masters the process.

Scientists have discovered that bek is an almost-perfect food. Corn is not, so now the Kipsigis are experiencing some deficiency diseases. They call them "diseases of corn" and seem to understand that they would not have them if they ate more bek.

When the Kipsigis have meat (mutton, goat, beef or chicken), they put whatever meat they have in a large aluminum pot with potatoes, cabbage, onions and lots of water and simmer it all day. They add seasonings to this, and it is quite tasty. They dip their gimyet in the broth, and that makes the gimyet taste much better.

The Kipsigis' favorite drink is sour milk flavored with charcoal. The women make it in dry, decorated gourd shells. The women decorate the gourds by burning a pattern onto the surface of the gourd – usually a sort of geometric pattern made of dots and short lines. The women add beaded leather carrying handles (I think they must glue these on somehow) and a beaded leather cap fastened to the gourd for safe keeping.

Before the woman fills the gourd with milk, she briefly rubs the insides of the gourd with a burning stick to clean it. She holds the gourd upside down and taps it to dislodge any large pieces of charcoal that might have broken off inside. Then she fills the gourd with fresh milk and sets it aside for a few days.

When she is ready to use the milk, she shakes the gourd vigorously and pours the milk into cups. The charcoal mixes with the sour milk for added flavor. The drink is called "mursik." Mursik has a bit of a bite to it because the milk has soured, and it is gritty because of the charcoal.

Frequently patients gave the nurses a gourd of mursik as a special thank you. We were to drink the mursik and return the gourd. I always drank at least one cupful of mursik from every thank-you gift but usually shared the rest of it with our houseboys. Our houseboys were young Kipsigis who wanted to earn money, and we missionaries needed help with the housework so we would have time to preach, teach and care for the sick.

I arrived in Kenya in August, so the missionary children were home from boarding school. Almost all the MKs in Kenya went to Rift Valley Academy, a school run by Africa Inland Mission and located about 20 miles north of Nairobi in a forested area near the edge of the Great Rift Valley. Their school year pretty much followed the American school year; the year began in September and was three months in school and one month at home. So the children were home April, August and December.

On the second day I was at Tenwek, one of the little MKs who was about 10 years old walked up to me and casually asked if I would like some fried ants. I don't think she got the reaction she was looking for. I looked at the ants in her frying pan and said, "No, thanks." Years later, I was a little disappointed that nobody ever offered me fried ants again. I think after about six months in Kenya, I would have been ready to try one.

Most of Tenwek Station as seen from across the river. The big building at the top is the secondary school. The next group of buildings includes the hospital. Next is missionary housing. The last two buildings are the Girls Boarding School (left) and the primary school. The church just above the river is not visible in this picture.

Tenwek Falls, a short distance north of the mission compound, now has a hydroelectric plant that supplies electricity twenty-four hours a day to Tenwek Station. The modern hospital now at Tenwek could not exist without continuous electrical power.

The grist mill by the falls.

These round, mud-and-wattle huts were the standard Kipsigis housing for most of the 1950s.

Pastor Zakayo Arap Sonoiya was Millie's language teacher.

Tenwek Falls as seen from a distance.

Kenya Glory, the colonial flower of Kenya, grows wild in the grasslands.

Tenwek Station is located about 30 miles south of the equator in the Kenya Highlands (about 8,000 feet above sea level).

CHAPTER TWO
My Kipsigis Sermon

I was a new missionary, having just recently completed my formal study of the Kipsigis language and passed the exam. I spent time every day at our little hospital learning the routines and responsibilities and practicing my new language by both listening and speaking. I had a fairly large vocabulary, and I could follow a conversation if I knew ahead of time what the main topic would be. I also had a pronounced American accent.

One day, Johana, one of the African elders, came into the nurses' office and was talking to Trudie Shryock, the older RN who had started the medical work at Tenwek years earlier.

They talked for a while, and then Trudie said to me, "Johana is supposed to have the service today, but he has a meeting and is looking for someone to do the service here; do you know of anyone who could do it?" I thought of the African pastors and knew I didn't know any of them well enough to suggest a substitute for Johana, so I told her, "No, I don't know of anyone."

They talked a little more, and then Trudie turned to me and said, "He thinks you should do it."

That was a startling thought! Although I had taught Sunday school, led devotions, and even delivered a sermon occasionally, I did not enjoy public speaking and had little confidence in myself to preach a sermon correctly. So I over-emphasized the situation by saying, "No, I can't preach in English much less in Kipsigis. I can't do it." Besides, for me to put together any kind of teaching took a lot of time, and time was running out.

Trudie relayed the message to Johana who frowned, pointed his finger at me and said emphatically, "The Lord will help you!" I not only understood his words, but also I knew in my heart that he was right. I had learned many memory verses that contained God's wonderful promises:

- "My strength is made perfect in weakness," II Cor. 12:9.
- "So shall my word be that goes forth from my mouth; it shall not return to me void, but it shall accomplish what I please, and it shall prosper in the thing for which I sent it," Isaiah 55:11.

I saw no room for further discussion, and I reluctantly agreed to speak at the service, which was scheduled to start in 45 minutes.

Johana left, promising to pray as he walked to his meeting, and I hurried down to the house to start working on my "sermon."

I chose Matthew 11:28-30 for my text: "Come to me, all you who labor and are heavy laden, and I will give you rest. Take my yoke upon you and learn from me, for I am gentle and lowly in heart, and you will find rest for your souls. For my yoke is easy and my burden is light."

The scripture seemed appropriate because more women than men were always at the hospital, and the Kipsigis women worked exceptionally hard. A Kipsigis woman's work included digging up the garden, planting it, tending it and bringing in the harvest. In addition, they brought water up from the river daily, gathered firewood, cooked meals over a little open fire, and washed the family clothes in the river. All this while being pregnant, nursing a little one, caring for a toddler and/or teaching the older children and adolescents of the family what they needed to know to be good Kipsigis.

With both my English Bible and Kipsigis Bible open before me, I wrote a short message in English and translated it into simple Kipsigis.

Even though I was planning to speak in Kipsigis, I asked one of the African nurses' aides to interpret for me because my American accent would be unfamiliar to most of the patients and their families.

The daily evangelistic services had been part of the hospital routine ever since the medical work began. At first the missionaries conducted them, but in 1950 there were sufficient African pastors, and they took turns speaking at the services. A grass-thatched pole building that was open on all sides had been constructed in the hospital area for this service. The patients and their family members sat on backless benches.

We sang some songs, and then I "preached" the "sermon." And even though my simple message was repeated, I think it took only 3-5 minutes, and then it was over.

The African nurses' aide invited anyone who wanted to accept Jesus as Savior – or even to learn more about Jesus - to stay in the shelter for prayer and dismissed the rest of the people. And that morning three women stayed for prayer! I marveled that the Lord could use me in His work of winning people to Himself. And even as I was surprised at the results of my Kipsigis "sermon," I realized that many others had contributed as well. Johana had prayed as he went to his meeting; Trudie had prayed because she knew how inadequate I felt; and possibly several people back in the States had prayed for me that morning because they took seriously their commitment to pray regularly for the missionaries whom they knew.

I did not know at the time that in a few years this incident would become one of my favorite experiences to share with people back in America. The story demonstrated so many things: our reason for being there as missionaries, the Lord's ability to use small things to accomplish His work, and the value of prayer. Thank you, Lord, for giving me this experience!

One of the daily evangelistic services in the pole building. During my second term, we built a cement block open-air chapel with real pews.

Almost anywhere the women walked, they were carrying something: a child or two, a gourd of mursik, laundry to wash in the river, firewood, grain to be ground, a big basket full of produce, produce for the offering at church, or five gallons of water balanced on their heads.

This woman has probably already carried her load of thatching grass for miles. When she arrives home, she will help her husband repair the thatching on their roof.

CHAPTER THREE
The Mau Mau Uprising

The year was 1952, and the news on the radio was bad. Terrorist activity was increasing around Nairobi. A small group from the Kikuyu tribe had begun attacking and killing Europeans, Christians and Loyalists. Loyalists were Africans working with, connected to or favoring the British colonial government of that day.

The news was especially bad because three of us missionaries were scheduled to leave after the noon meal to go to Nairobi for some government-sponsored meetings. Bob Smith, the superintendent of our mission, was going. Alice Day, a teacher, was to represent our educational program, and I was to represent our medical work. We talked the situation over and decided we would go anyway in spite of the news.

Kenya had been placed under military rule. I didn't know exactly what that meant but thought it might include stricter laws, less freedom, inconveniences and maybe even some degree of danger. What it really meant was that we would see a much more noticeable military presence as regiments from other parts of the Commonwealth were brought in to help keep the peace. Because we were way out in the bush, we never saw any military presence unless we were in one of the larger cities. I once saw the Black Watch Regiment from Scotland. Their dress uniforms were kilts made from the beautiful Black Watch tartan – a checkerboard of small blue and green blocks.

We left Tenwek in the early afternoon because Alice had to teach in the morning. We planned to stop for the night a little short of halfway to Nairobi. Our progress was slow because we encountered several police road blocks along the way. The police searched each vehicle for Africans traveling south who might be wanting to join the Kikuyu in their rebellion against English rule.

We arrived at our destination in plenty of time for the evening meal – we even had time to check into our hotel rooms before dinner.

The Londiani Hotel was a fair-sized hotel to stand alone in a forested area. But it seemed to be doing well judging by the number of people who were there that evening. Only a few tables remained empty in the dining room.

Tension in the dining room was noticeable especially among the African waiters. They were on the alert and frequently talked to each other. They constantly watched the main entrance to the dining room as though they expected trouble. And they hurried through their tasks, apparently anxious to leave and go home to their families.

The tension spread to the guests: Certainly we felt it. Almost everyone ate quickly and departed to the safety of a locked room.

Bob walked Alice and me back to our room and continued down the hall to his. We locked our door, and because we had nothing else to do and we were tired, we got ready for bed. Although the hour was still early, we were ready to retire at 9:00. Just then, we heard a light knock on our door.

"Who is it?" Alice asked.

"It's me, Bob. Let me in," came the answer in Bob's familiar voice.

Alice opened the door, and in walked Bob with his sleeping bag, his pillow and his gun!

He said, "I'm spending the night here," and proceeded to spread out his sleeping bag on the floor between the two single beds in the room.

We were a little surprised but under the circumstances did not object. Protection sounded good in case of an attack.

I slept well and woke up the following morning at 6:00. Alice was up and almost dressed. "Bob left about five," she said. "He woke me up so I could lock the door again."

After breakfast we drove on to Nairobi and our meetings. Then a couple of days later, we returned to Tenwek. We left early and made the trip in one day.

Police road blocks were still present, but the trip back was without incident.

Because the English had so many colonies, they had had lots of experience dealing with rebellions and knew just what to do. They started by declaring military rule and by isolating the rebels as much as possible to keep other tribes from becoming involved.

Almost immediately the government sent guidelines for staying alive in areas where the terrorists were active. My guess is that the government sent the guidelines all over Kenya because they didn't know how quickly or how far the Mau Mau movement would spread.

And to the Africans the government gave little pre-set radios so they could keep all the other tribes informed about what was going on. My memory tells me that the government gave one radio per family, but that seems cost prohibitive. So I'm going to amend my memory and say that the radios were given to every chief and sub-chief, and they were to share the news with all the men in the area. Probably the broadcasts were in Swahili, the trade language of Kenya.

A few weeks after coming back from Nairobi, I was definitely feeling the tension of the whole situation. I had known before I came to Kenya that something like this might happen, but I had not expected to feel the way I did. I was afraid and wishing I weren't in Kenya; concentration was hard. Before I left America, I had declared my faith in the Lord, and now I wondered why my faith had been so easily shaken.

One afternoon I had a little free time. I walked upstairs to my room, went in, and closed the door. I stopped a few steps into the room and just stood there. Satan was there with his accusations, and the Lord was also there.

Satan said, "Now look what you've done! You are out here and will probably be killed, and you haven't accomplished anything yet!"

"I will be with you and protect you," the Lord answered.

Sarcastically, Satan said, "Well, missionaries have been killed, you know!"

In a gentle voice the Lord said, "If that is what I choose for you, then I will give you grace for whatever happens."

Satan, the liar, tried one more time: "But your parents won't understand!"

God quietly responded, "If I can give you grace when you need it, I can give your parents grace as well."

That short conversation with God was a turning point for me; my faith was restored, and I knew that my loving Heavenly Father was watching over me as well as over all the other missionaries who were working in Kenya. I could take my lantern in the middle of the night and go up the hill to the hospital without fear. God's presence was very real during those unsettling times.

CHAPTER FOUR
Under Military Rule

A small village named Uplands had been established just outside of Nairobi for the Loyalist soldiers and their families. Roughly six months after the beginning of the Mau Mau uprising, the news was disturbing once again.

One day while the Uplands men were out on patrol, the Mau Mau made an unusual daytime attack and killed almost all of the people who were in the village at the time – women, children and old men. Few survived to give eye-witness accounts of the atrocities. The Mau Mau brutally killed some children in front of their mothers.

To the Kipsigis and the Masai, the killing of women, children and old men was nothing more than an act of cowardice. If they had been interested in joining the Mau Mau before, they certainly weren't now after hearing the news of the massacre.

The Masai took action: They held a council meeting, voted and sent word to the governor that if he would give them permission, they would go in and wipe out the entire Kikuyu tribe. The governor said, "Thanks, but no thanks," and, to their credit, the Masai let the matter drop.

The Kipsigis just sort of shook their heads and lost all interest in the Mau Mau, and I think that was true of most other tribes in Kenya.

The Uplands Massacre was a big strategy mistake on the part of the Mau Mau and marked the beginning of the end for them.

• • •

In early February, 1952, Princess Elizabeth and Prince Philip came to Kenya for a short visit. Maisie, the mission bookkeeper, and I happened to be in Nairobi when the Prince and Princess arrived, and we were staying at a small hotel on the route that the royal motorcade would be taking from the airport to wherever they were staying – probably the New Stanley Hotel or the governor's mansion. Our hotel management had posted the expected time for the motorcade to pass, so we two Americans were by the road in plenty of time to see the English princess. We were the only spectators at the place where we were waiting.

The motorcade was short but not the least bit disappointing. Princess Elizabeth and Prince Philip rode in an open convertible, and the princess sat on the side nearest to where we were standing. So we got a good look at her. She was only about 10 feet from us, smiling and waving to us! She was young and beautiful, and we were thrilled to see her so close.

One of the places the couple visited while in Kenya was the Tree-Top Hotel, a big tree house (with beds for napping) above a busy water-hole in the game reserve. Floodlights allowed guests to watch the animals come and go all night long.

A few days after we had seen Princess Elizabeth and after we returned to Tenwek, we heard that Elizabeth's father, George VI, had died. By the time we got the news, the new queen was well on her way back to London.

Only a few weeks later, the Mau Mau destroyed the Tree-Top Hotel. Their action was a clear statement that they disliked foreign rulers and wished them gone.

• • •

Because of the altitude at Tenwek (between 7 thousand and 8 thousand feet above sea level) a doctor had advised that each missionary go down to sea level for at least 2 weeks every 2 years. Maisie and I were on such a leave sometime in the early 1950s during the time the Mau Mau were still in revolt.

We were at a resort on the Indian Ocean south of Mombasa, Kenya's biggest seaport. While there, we met a young English girl. She was recuperating from a serious illness and also was supposed to spend time at sea level. Her name was Ezmee (Ez-may), and she was about my age, not quite 30. She had a 5-year-old son named Michael. She missed him a lot and told stories of his adventures. She and her husband owned a farm at the 14,000-foot level. The only place I can think of in Kenya where a farm would be at that altitude would be the foothills of Mt. Kenya. She said they could raise temperate fruit there such as peaches and apples.

Although we had an abundance of tropical fruit at Tenwek, and I enjoyed eating it almost every day, I missed some of the temperate fruits, especially peaches and grapes. I don't remember what kind of farming Ezmee and her husband did there, but just the fact that they could have a peach tree and a few grape vines sounded awfully good to me.

Ezmee also was a doctor. She held regular clinics for the Africans in her area. She charged them a small fee, and her prices were similar to ours at Tenwek. So that was a real service for the Africans.

Ezmee, Maisie and I got along well and enjoyed spending time together. We played in the warm ocean, hiked up and down the beaches, looked for sea shells, ate our meals together in the dining room and got beautiful tans. Then it was time for Maisie and me to return to Tenwek. Ezmee was to stay for a short while longer.

We exchanged addresses and fully expected to write occasionally and exchange Christmas cards. But about four months later we heard on the news one evening that Ezmee and her family had all been killed by the Mau Mau.

Those investigating the murders pieced the events together this way: Both Ezmee and her husband were ambushed – he when he went out to lock up and check to see that everything was as it should be, and she when she went looking for him because he had not returned in good time. Their bodies were found fairly close together. Then the attackers went in the house, killed the African guard who was stationed outside Michael's bedroom door (possibly a fellow tribesman), and then entered the bedroom and killed Michael. All of the deaths appeared to have been quick.

So Ezmee became the only person I knew who was killed by the Mau Mau. I have thought of her and her family often through the years. I'm sorry Ezmee and her husband didn't get to grow old together and that they never got to see Michael as an adult. I'm sorry for the grandparents back in England. I'm sorry Michael didn't get to live his life and fulfill most of his dreams. And I'm sorry for the African guard and for his family who mourned for him and experienced great loss for years to come.

I'm sorry our friendship was cut short, and Maisie and I never got to meet Ezmee's family and visit their farm. I'm sorry the clinics for the Africans had to end because the doctor was no longer available.

A beach on the Indian Ocean near Mombasa. Notice the white breakers in the distance; these mark the site of a coral reef that protects the coastal waters from sharks and makes swimming in the area safe.

CHAPTER FIVE
Forgetting the Guidelines

About halfway through my first term, we opened another station, Cheptenye, about 50 miles from Tenwek and only 11 miles from Kericho. I was assigned to go to Cheptenye and open a dispensary.

Five of us were to be on the station. Loren and Lois Clark and their two-year-old son, John, were to live in the main part of the house. Hazel Evans, the teacher, and I were to share an upstairs apartment.

The station itself covered about 5 acres and was almost flat. The house stood at the top of the property and the dispensary at the very bottom. The property had a slight slope down from the house – not very noticeable, but if a car were left out of gear and the brakes not on, it would slowly roll away. The school building and the church were at the top of the property across from the house.

With just a dispensary to run and two African nurses' aides to help me, I had time to teach. I taught eighth grade geometry and a health class and helped with the women's work. I enjoyed all of these activities.

The colonial government assessed and improved roads all over Kenya. Our road between Tenwek and Kericho was greatly improved to assure the government could transport troops and military equipment quickly and safely and that anyone with severe injuries from an attack could be evacuated easily if that ever became necessary.

In addition, the government also enrolled all medical personnel working in Kenya in case they ever needed to draft us to help. I became Enrolled Nurse #13. Thankfully, none of us ever were called up.

The colonial government had put out guidelines for the safety of those living in areas where the Mau Mau were active. All of us got copies of these guidelines in case the danger spread to our area.

The guidelines were practical: Keep your drapes closed after dark so you will not be an easy target; rearrange your furniture frequently so the enemy cannot even guess where you might be sitting on the other side of the drapes; do not let Africans walk behind you – keep them in front of you where you can see what they are doing; be suspicious of all Africans – Mau Mau members will try to get your trust, and then when the opportunity presents itself, they will attack.

These were guidelines, but I had a tendency to think of them as rules. Then, if I forgot one of them, I felt guilty, especially if forgetting got me in trouble or in danger, no matter how temporary.

Let me tell you about three times I forgot the guidelines. All three of these happened after I transferred to Cheptenye Station to open the dispensary.

My first story occurred only a few months after I moved to Cheptenye.

Running a dispensary was much easier than the work at the hospital had been. We took care of out-patients only. If anyone needed to be hospitalized, the government hospital was only eleven miles away in Kericho. Rarely was I called out at night.

But one night Hazel, the teacher with whom I shared the apartment, woke me up. She said that Arap Tanu, our night watchman, and one of the African pastors were outside calling me. She had heard them calling; I had slept right through it. I talked to the men from my upstairs window. The pastor's wife was sick again and wanted more of the medicine I had given her a few weeks earlier.

I remembered her and knew what she needed, so I agreed to go down to the dispensary and get it for her. Quickly I put on socks and shoes, threw my coat over my pajamas, grabbed my keys and a big flashlight and hurried outside.

The pastor said he would go home and get the money for the medicine. As you can imagine, I wanted to get back to bed as quickly as possible, so I took off running toward the dispensary. The slight downward slope of the property made running easy.

About halfway down, I heard the clomp, clomp of oversized boots and the labored breathing of Arap Tanu. I slowed down a bit, thinking Arap Tanu shouldn't be running like that – he'll have a heart attack. And then I thought, Millie, you are breaking a rule: Not only do you have an African running behind you, but you have an African *with a spear* running behind you!

What do I do now? Just keep going, and don't act afraid, I answered myself. As we approached the dispensary, I could find no credible reason for me to be afraid of or to distrust Arap Tanu.

He was the loveable grandfatherly type. He had served as a Kenyan policeman until relatively recently; then after he retired, he returned to his Kipsigis birthplace and sometime later applied for the job as our night watchman. With all his training and experience, he seemed perfect for the job.

He held his flashlight so I could see to unlock the door. Then, after I went inside the dispensary, he stood in the doorway, nearly filling it as he rested his arms on the doorposts and caught his breath.

He watched me and what I was doing, but he also was constantly checking the area surrounding the dispensary, looking and listening and frequently turning to see or hear better.

After I finished, I locked up, and we walked back up the slope together. The pastor returned to the house about the same time we did. We took care of business, said our thank-yous and good nights, and all went our separate ways.

As I drifted off to sleep again, I reviewed the events of the last hour. The guidelines were good and were given for our safety. But being suspicious of every African who crossed one's path was a stifling way to live. I believed that Arap Tanu had accompanied me to the dispensary for my protection, and all his actions had proved that was true.

Another time I put myself in jeopardy was when I discovered our houseboy standing on our porch at nine o'clock at night.

"Why are you still here?" I asked.

"It's raining," he said in a way that made it sound like, "Can't you *see* that it's raining?"

Yes, it *was* raining, and if he was going to sit there until it quit, he just might be there a long time. So I offered to drive him home. I knew where he lived. His home was right off the mission station, close to the church. So I couldn't get lost.

After telling Hazel where I was going, we took off. As we left the station, our houseboy started giving me directions.

"Don't you live right here next to Cheptenye?" I asked.

"Yes, but I'm going to a friend's house."

"How far is that?"

"Not far," he answered; so I kept on driving.

The trip to his friend's house truly was short. He jumped out and ran in out of the rain.

I turned the Land Rover around and started to follow my tracks back. Soon, I was going by a cornfield I was sure we had not passed as we came. This corn was taller than what we had seen earlier. And then I came to the edge of a gully I had never seen before. At this point, the gully was uncrossable by vehicle.

I turned around, drove past the tall corn again and stopped. My sense of direction had vanished. I had no idea which way to drive to get back to Cheptenye Station although I knew it was close – an easy little walk – if I just knew which way to go. Nor did I know how to get back to the hut where I had just let our houseboy off.

Too late. I could see now that I should have let him off to run the rest of the way to his friend's house as soon as he told me that was where he was going. Then I would have known how to get back to the station.

Now what were my options? Best to stay with the Land Rover. I could keep the lights on to mark my location as long as I had petrol, but I probably didn't have enough to last the night – sunrise was about eight-and-a-half hours away. The Land Rover had a roof but was open on the sides above the doors. The running motor offered a little heat. The air would be uncomfortably cold by morning – maybe even down in the 40s, and I wasn't dressed for that. Periodically I honked the horn, hoping someone friendly would hear it, come and point me in the right direction.

And what were the dangers of being alone all night in an open Land Rover? I thought of the Mau Mau and decided I faced little threat there. As I said, our tribe disliked their method of operation and had decided against participation long ago. But an isolated member could be here or there. And if any were in the area, this was a perfect set-up.

No large predatory animals lived in our area, so I didn't need to worry about that. We had seen snakes occasionally, but they were usually not out at night.

My biggest threat was probably from dogs African families owned. Dogs in Kenya are racist. If Africans own them, they have a strong dislike for Europeans and vice versa. I think each race has a distinct smell because of their distinct diets, and that's what sets the dogs off. If the local families let their dogs out at night, I could be in serious danger.

And what would I do if I needed to go to the bathroom?

Next I looked at the likelihood of my still being stranded in the Land Rover when the sun came up. Very unlikely. Hazel knew where I had gone, and unless she had fallen asleep right after I left, she would not retire until I was safely home. And if I didn't return in a reasonable time, she would alert the night watchman and Loren Clark, the only man on our station. They would come looking for me. I decided to keep the motor running and the lights on for at least another hour – unless I ran out of petrol.

I had turned the headlights out briefly a couple of times just to see how I would do. The moon was not shining, and I saw few stars. Rain was still falling. The darkness was intense. It seemed to push at me from all sides and demand that I stay in the vehicle. My biggest fear was I would panic and do something foolish. Maybe the darkness would be my friend and encourage me to stay in the Land Rover and wait quietly.

As I thought through my situation, I sent quick little prayers to my Heavenly Father – prayers for protection and prayers for help, prayers for someone to direct me back to the station. And somewhere along the way, I started to cry.

But now having made the decision to expect help, I started praying more earnestly. I prayed with my eyes open, watching for any movement in the surrounding area. The night sounds were consistent, actually soft and comforting. Suddenly I was aware of a flash of light off to my right. Lightning? No! There it was again, bobbing along. Someone coming with a flashlight? It would appear so. That was funny. I thought Cheptenye was to my left! And very soon Arap Tanu, our night watchman, stepped into the circle of light my headlights created. I was so happy to see him I could have hugged him – but that would have embarrassed him. He was smiling as he climbed into the passenger seat, but he noticed my tear-stained face, gave an embarrassed little chuckle and said to me in English, "Misi Rosiman, why you cry?"

I don't know that I ever gave him an answer; I thanked him for coming and asked him, "Which way?" He started pointing, and I started driving again. Soon we were going through the gate and onto Cheptenye Station. Hazel had put 3 candles in my window to help guide me back. Unfortunately, they had been invisible from where I was waiting.

She had tea ready. How thoughtful, refreshing and warming that was!

Thank you, Lord, for the safety of home. And thank you that once again my trust in Arap Tanu had not been misplaced!

My third mistake was not so much a breaking of the government guidelines as it was breaking one of my own rules. I had made it a practice to never go into an unknown area alone. I took someone I already knew and trusted, and usually that was someone who also spoke Kipsigis. That person could be a Kipsigis or an American as long as he or she knew the area.

One day I had driven from Cheptenye to Kericho by myself on an errand, a short trip of 11 miles one way. As I was returning to Cheptenye, about halfway there, a couple of men were standing along the road waving at me to stop. When I stopped, they said, "We've been looking for you. There is a woman who is very sick and needs to go to the hospital. Can you take her?"

"Where is she?" I asked

"At home. We'll show you. Can you take her?"

I agreed and invited the men to get in the Land Rover. Soon we turned off the road and were traveling on pastureland, uphill and down. And I realized what I had done. I was in an unfamiliar area with no special landmarks with two Kipsigis men whom I had never seen before. They kept telling me our destination was just a little further. I began to pray and ask for the Lord's protection during the trip.

Finally they told me to stop by some thorn bushes. I pulled the Land Rover up to where I could look down a hill between two hedges of thorn bushes. Nothing was down there except more pasture.

"Where is the woman?" I asked.

"She's down there; come with us," they assured me.

The men got out and started down the hill. I kind of dragged my feet, wanting to stay close to the Land Rover in case I needed it.

They kept turning around, beckoning to me and saying, "Come."

Finally I realized I was too far from the Land Rover to make a quick getaway and decided I might as well just keep praying and go on.

After the men walked around the end of the hedge, I heard voices. As I rounded the hedge, I saw a hut, and outside in the sunshine, lying on a cowhide, I saw a very sick woman. I was glad to see her and to know that this trip was indeed a trip of mercy. The men carried her up the hill, using the cowhide as a stretcher. We loaded her into the back of the Land Rover and headed for Kericho and the government hospital.

After that foray into the countryside, I was late getting home, but the others at Cheptenye were only a little worried. The two men had come to Cheptenye earlier looking for a ride to the hospital, and the mission staff had told them I had gone to Kericho and soon would be traveling back along the road between Kericho and Cheptenye.

CHAPTER SIX
First Furlough

I came home on my first homeland leave (about two years in the States) in December of 1954. Needless to say, I was excited. I was especially anxious to see my parents. Dad had turned 61 in August, and Mother would be 60 in November. I had aged a bit, too. I would be 30 in November. And my sister had her first daughter while I was gone. A two-year-old would be fun! I joyfully looked forward to seeing my family and friends. I wanted to see all the old familiar places: the farm; my church in Beaverton; the high school in Hillsboro; Cascade College, the Christian College I had attended in Portland; and Emanuel Hospital, also in Portland, where I had taken my nurse's training.

I wanted to see frost and maybe snow again; I wanted to see the seasons change – and not just from wet to dry. I wanted to celebrate all the American holidays, and I wanted to hear American spoken again.

I knew I was going to have to speak in many churches to raise money to go back. The thought of having to do this frightened me. I still felt like a new missionary with limited knowledge and expertise. The work had been pretty routine – very little that was exciting or interesting had happened. I was unsure as to what I would say when I had to talk about the mission work in Kenya.

The days before leaving Kenya were busy. I packed up my belongings, put my things in storage and cleaned out my room for a new occupant. I wore and/or packed my warmest clothes. Not having a winter coat, I wore the warmest coat I had, a light spring coat, and hoped that the vehicles in which I would be riding during the last half of my trip would be heated and only a short walk from the waiting rooms.

I don't remember details of my departure from Nairobi, but I do know that nobody warned me that after 4 ½ years overseas, I would find myself adjusting to my own culture! My first surprise happened as we landed in London. We landed there about 4:00 p.m. on a December afternoon, and low in the west in a slightly misty sky I saw a small, pale sun. I hadn't seen a winter sun for five years and had forgotten what one looked like.

The second surprise came in Iceland. We landed at Reykjavik about 2:00 a.m. for refueling and had the opportunity to go into the airport restaurant. The place was crowded with young and somewhat rowdy American soldiers. I was so disappointed in the sound of the American language! After hearing the King's English spoken for four years, American English sounded awfully flat! And I hated the thought that I probably sounded just like those soldiers.

After a couple more stops, we arrived a half hour early in Portland, Oregon, at 11:40 p.m. My light coat had been adequate because we were never out in the weather for long. My folks were at the airport to meet the plane. What a joy to see them! When we got home, our dog didn't recognize me and growled at me. I guess I still smelled like Africa!

During my time in Kenya, I had become so used to the African church services that I was unprepared for an American service. An African service was usually an hour-and-a-half long – sometimes longer. Time was an unimportant factor to the Africans. In Africa I was used to the hymn number being announced before each song, and time was given for people to find the right page. But in our church in Beaverton, the hymn numbers were listed in the bulletin and everyone, except me, had found the words before the organ started to play. I finally caught on by the end of the service, and I remembered that we had done our services that way for a long time. The next week I followed the plan just like an American!

Another thing that surprised me was the winter coats on the animals I saw outside. Their coats looked shaggy as if they needed a good brushing, but I remembered that this happened in winter in Oregon because of the seasonal changes.

On Christmas morning we had an unusual light dusting of snow. I felt that the Lord had sent that especially for me as a welcome-home message.

During the holiday season, I visited with friends and family, neighbors and classmates. Everybody had questions: What were the Kenyans like? What did they eat? What did you eat? What did they wear? What were their homes like? What were the roads like? Were the people responsive to the Gospel?

One of the girls from my nursing class asked, "Are the people very primitive?" I didn't know how to answer that, so I described a Kipsigis house. Her response startled me. She said, "Gee, they are primitive, aren't they?" I had to think about that for a while before I could admit that the Kipsigis were "primitive," and I wondered how in only 4 ½ years I could have come to accept their lifestyle as normal and ordinary – nothing unusual, nothing interesting about it. The questions and the conversations I had during those early days at home helped me know what people were interested in and gave me ideas of what to share when I was the missionary speaker.

Many times someone asked me to say a few words in Kipsigis. I usually quoted John 3:16 and finished by saying that those words say the same thing to the Kipsigis that John 3:16 in English says to us.

Although public speaking was still not my favorite thing to do, I enjoyed it more than I thought I would because people were interested, they wanted to support missionaries, and they wanted to pray for the missionaries and the people with whom they were working.

Part of the time, when I didn't have meetings during my furlough, I rented a room near Emanuel Hospital and worked. Being again in a modern hospital and seeing the changes that had occurred while I was away was good for me. I had to brush up on my medical vocabulary because in Kenya I usually thought in simple English and spoke in simple Kipsigis.

The mission had asked me to take midwifery training before returning to Kenya; so in August of 1956, I flew to London and became a student midwife at the Salvation Army Mother's Hospital in East London. I already had one friend at the hospital, a young nurse from Denmark, Greta Andersen, who had worked in Oregon and attended Cascade College in Portland. I had met her several times soon after I got home. Because we were both "foreigners" in London, and because we were the two oldest student midwives there, we became good friends. She already had finished Part One of the training and was starting Part Two when I arrived to start Part One.

The first six months of training consisted of classes, ward duty and a prescribed number of deliveries that we did under supervision. In Part Two, we were "on district." Two or three student midwives lived in a home with a district midwife. We held clinics in our home and did the deliveries in the patients' homes. To get to our patients' homes, we traveled by bicycle with our bag of supplies and a wrapped bedpan strapped on the back of the bike.

My first patient in Part One was in isolation because of an infection, and she spoke with a pronounced Cockney accent. I, too, spoke with a pronounced accent, so we had trouble understanding each other at first. But we managed.

Between Parts One and Two was a two-week break, and Greta sent me home to her parents in Aarhus, Denmark. They spoke no English, and I spoke no Danish, but they had an English-Danish dictionary and a Danish-English dictionary. So we got along great. I had a good time with them and am glad I had that time in Denmark.

The final midwifery exam was oral and lasted ten or fifteen minutes. A doctor and a midwife, both well-experienced, were the examiners. Each student had written up a "case book" on ten or so of the deliveries she had done in Part One. The examiners looked at that book and asked about those cases or about any other subject we had been taught in the year of training. Needless to say, I was scared. I wanted to get back to Kenya, and I would have much rather written my answers on paper than give them orally.

When I was called in for my examination, I handed the examiners my book and waited until I was told to sit before I sat down (as we had been instructed to do). Our training had been good, and I knew the answers to the questions they asked. After a while, the examiners relaxed and started to "visit." They asked what part of America I was from and what I was going to do now. And when my time was up, I knew I had passed! Confirmation came by post a week or so later.

And then I was back to Kenya for a second term.

I was to be at Tenwek again and work at the hospital. The one big change I noticed was that Kenya was no longer under military rule because the Mau Mau were no longer active.

As the number of active terrorists became fewer and the attacks decreased, the government forces were able to round up those who had been involved and put them in a separate facility between Nairobi and Mombasa. It was my understanding that this was something like a concentration camp. The government brought in special counselors to rehabilitate the ex-terrorists and prepare them for productive lives in their own culture. Missionaries who spoke the Kikuyu language were invited to help with the rehabilitation. I don't know if any of the former terrorists were ever convicted of crimes or spent time in jail.

One day one of the missionaries asked one of the former terrorists, "Why did you not attack Rift Valley Academy?"

"Oh, we tried," he replied. "The first night we got lost in the forest and ended up at the railway station" (it was five miles away from the school). "And the second time, we got within sight of the school compound, but we didn't dare attack."

"Why not?"

"Because the school was surrounded by soldiers in gleaming white uniforms! They were tall and carried large swords, and we did not dare attack."

So the terrorists turned around and went home. They never tried to attack Rift Valley Academy again.

Because the Africans kept no record of dates, we don't know what night the sighting of the angels took place. And because none of the fathers have come forth with added information, we can assume that the fathers who were guarding the school that fateful night saw nothing unusual and were totally unaware of the extra "guards" who were visible only to the terrorists.

The Lord not only protected the children by sending His angels, but He also protected the volunteer guards – the fathers – and kept them from having to shoot an African, which would have been devastating for a missionary. We praise God for His protection.

Millie at her graduation from midwifery training.

Millie and her bike ready to go see a patient.
Note the little black bag and the wrapped bedpan.

The Salvation Army's Mothers' Hospital in London is where Millie did her midwifery training.

Nairobi Airport is located between Nairobi and the Nairobi Game Reserve.

CHAPTER SEVEN
John Clark

In mid-December, the dry season was beginning to turn the hills brown in the Highlands of Kenya. Although December and January were the hottest months of the year, the Kipsigis people did not plant their gardens at that time – not because of the heat but because of the lack of moisture.

When I first got to Kenya, I was surprised to find that the Kipsigis people, living 30 miles south of the Equator, planted their corn about the same time my Dad planted his corn in Oregon. Their harvest took place a little later than the harvest in Oregon because Dad's corn was for the fresh market and the Kipsigis let their corn ripen on the stalk and dry so it would keep even through the rainy seasons. Corn was a big part of their diet.

Christmas during the hot, dry weather was an adjustment for all of us from America. I remember being a little homesick in 1950, my first Christmas in Kenya. Then a couple days before Christmas, Trudie Shryock, the nurse in charge of the medical work, gave me the job of wrapping some little gifts for the African nurses' aides, and one of the other missionaries had set up a loudspeaker and was playing Christmas carols across Tenwek station. Those two things made me feel like it was Christmas in spite of the weather and the Easter lilies blooming in our garden!

Now I was well into my second term in Kenya and had adjusted to the climate and cultural changes that went along with the holiday. Only two of us were living in the single ladies' home – Eva Gilger, the principal of the secondary school, and me. Eva liked to make decisions and get things done early, so she had been looking for a Christmas tree. No fir trees were available, but at a distance the wattle trees looked usable. A local family owned a grove of wattle trees a few miles from Tenwek. Eva had seen one tree that had a nice top and had arranged for the tree to be cut down and the top 6 or 7 feet of the tree to be cut off and sold to us for a few shillings to be our Christmas tree. The remainder of the long trunk eventually would be sawed into lumber.

So that afternoon, although it was still early in the month, we drove to get our tree. Sure enough, the tree had been cut as promised, but when we looked for our Christmas tree, we found that all the branches had been lopped off except for the top six or seven inches!

Eva called to the owner who quickly responded, "I know, I know. The workmen did not understand. Pick out another tree, and we will cut it for you."

So we picked out a tree, and they cut it and sold us the top six feet – branches and all. We took our tree home, set it up and decorated it that evening before we retired. Freedom Hall had a nice supply of Christmas decorations that various members of the household had donated. We were almost ready for Christmas!

• • •

The next day was December 16, and at about 10:00 in the morning while I was working at the hospital, one of the nurses' aides came and said Mr. Lewton was calling me from the road above the hospital. As I came around the building, he called out, "Millie, go down to the house."

"Why? What's wrong?" I asked.

"Just go down to the house now!" he called back as he sped away, leaving a small cloud of dust hanging in the air.

All I could think was that a European must need medical attention – someone who should be seen in one of the residences instead of the hospital setting. So I grabbed my stethoscope and hurried down to our house.

When I got there, the missionaries already were gathering. It is strange, but I cannot remember whether we were inside or outside as we heard the news from Gene Lewton.

He had been down at the Indian shops when a call came from our Jebulungu Station, twenty-five miles away, asking the Indians to get a message to Tenwek as quickly as possible. Because Gene was there, he was able to take the message himself. Six-year-old John Clark, adopted son of Loren and Lois Clark (our missionaries assigned to the Jebulungu Station), had fallen into the river about an hour earlier, and no one had yet found the body. They hoped to recover the body soon and come to Tenwek that day and have the funeral the next morning.

Gene and some of the other men were going to Jebulungu to help with the recovery. The rest of us would start preparations for the funeral and for overnight guests.

After sharing the news with our houseboys and with the African nurses, I tried to work. Concentrating was hard. I had known Loren and Lois for four years in college. Part of the time Lois' room was just a few doors from mine. I was experiencing what I considered to be a type of denial. Six or eight times that day my subconscious mind came up with a solution to the unacceptable situation we were facing. With a triumphant burst of confidence, my mind suggested that we go back and start the day over and not let this happen. For about ten seconds, I felt some relief; then I realized that was not possible. What had happened had happened, and it was going to make a difference for the rest of our lives. Somehow I needed to adjust to that.

Loren and Lois had adopted John as an infant after they came to Kenya. He was a Caucasian baby who needed a family. He had turned six in November.

Several years earlier John gave us all a scare because he was not speaking – putting words together – as much as he should have done for his age. Then when he was three, he started speaking in three languages – English, Kipsigis and Swahili. He kept the languages separate, using only words of one language as he spoke. And he knew what language each person around him spoke; so he was able to converse with each person appropriately.

A few months before John died, when the children were home from boarding school, the older children held a Vacation Bible School for the younger ones. John came home from that one day all excited and told his mother that he had accepted Jesus as his Savior.

• • •

As I recall, the caravan arrived from Jebulungu around 3:00 p.m. bringing John's body and the missionaries and their families from that station. We chose to lay the body out in the nurses' classroom, a small frame building on the hospital grounds. Because I was the only nurse assigned to Tenwek at the time, taking care of the body was my responsibility.

Before Gene left the building, he picked up the corner of one of the hospital sheets and asked if he could have that to line the casket. I hesitated before giving him permission because our hospital sheets had been made out of unbleached muslin, and that seemed inappropriate for a casket lining. But I didn't have any nice white material to use, and I doubted that any of the others did, either. So that sheet was probably our best choice. I looked at it again. It was old and had been laundered many times. (Yes, the hospital had an electric washing machine.) After being laundered, the sheets were spread on the grass to dry. And now that sheet was no longer unbleached but was bleached to a white white and was velvety soft. So I told Gene to take it for the casket.

Lois had brought fresh clothes for John to wear. I cleaned him up and dressed the body. I don't remember what we did with the clothes John had been wearing, but I remember emptying his pockets and taking the things down to his mother. She said that she didn't want them – just give them away. So I did. I gave myself the little knife that John had been carrying, and I still have it. Every time I see it, I rub the smooth metal surface, open the blades and remember John. The memory of him brings a smile to my face.

After I finished at the hospital, I went to the shop where several of the people were working on the casket. Dr. Probst from the African Inland Mission station about 45 miles away had heard the news and had come to see if he could be of any help. He had experience with burials in the tropics. I arrived just in time to hear him say, "It's one of those things that if it's done right, nobody will notice, but if it's done wrong, everybody will notice." I watched for a few minutes, but they didn't need my help at the shop, so I went on to my house for the evening meal.

The missionaries decided to have the funeral in our living room because that was the largest room in any of the residences. The funeral was scheduled for 10:00 a.m. the next morning. That would give the missionaries from Cheptenye and the Bible School time to arrive.

At one point Lois came into our living room and looked around. Our Christmas tree seemed out of place in view of what had happened that day. I told her we would take the tree down for the service, but she said, "No, no, no. John loved Christmas and was so looking forward to it. Just leave it where it is." So we did.

That night I went to bed at my usual time but could not sleep. Finally I got up, lit my lantern and walked out to the garden and picked flowers. Some of the other missionaries were still working on the casket in the shop. After an hour or so I had enough flowers for several nice bouquets I could put together in the morning. Picking the flowers relaxed me, and then I was able to go to sleep.

I slept well until 5:00 a.m. When I woke up, I thought about the funeral and wondered how the body looked now. Suddenly I had a frightening thought. The classroom provided protection from most predators, but what about the soldier ants? They could enter the building through very small openings, and they could do a lot of damage! I threw on my cape over my pajamas, lit my lantern and hurried to the hospital.

As I entered the building, I watched carefully for ants, but, thankfully, I saw none. And John's body was in perfect condition. I went back to the house to start the day in a more routine sort of way and had time to fix the bouquets.

At 8:00 a.m. we transferred the body to the casket, and at that time the body was already showing signs of deterioration. We called together the missionaries who had been at Tenwek overnight and had a short viewing period. Then we sealed the casket.

Loren and Lois had decided to have the burial in the Tenwek churchyard. They chose a place on the south side of the church in the corner between two wings of the church. This was to be the first grave – the first cemetery at Tenwek.

After the site was selected, the workmen dug the grave. To my knowledge, none of us thought to thank the Lord that we had never needed a cemetery before. The mission had been founded in 1895 and turned over to World Gospel Mission in the early '30s. For sixty years no one had needed a cemetery.

The missionaries from the other two stations arrived in good time for the service. They were disappointed the casket had been sealed, and they could not have a parting look at John. But they understood why.

Jerry Fish, who was our acting superintendent at the time, spoke at the service. He mentioned that John in his short life had been greatly loved. Now he would be number one in the new cemetery, and he would always be number one there. And even though he was just a child, he would be greatly missed.

Most of the missionaries returned to their stations that day or the next morning. But Loren and Lois stayed at Tenwek for a few more days. Several times I saw them walking hand-in-hand down the hill to visit the new grave.

At one point Lois asked me where we got the satin for the casket. I had to tell her it wasn't satin, just a white sheet. But I thought that those who prepared the casket must have done it right because even the mother didn't notice that the lining was just muslin.

Because Christmas was near, Lois made a comparison. She said God was willing to let His Son leave heaven and come to a sinful earth, and now her son had left the sinful earth and gone to a wonderful heaven, and she could be happy about that.

Christmas was hard for all of us that year but especially for Loren and Lois. Packages kept arriving from the States with gifts for John. Lois opened them and immediately distributed the clothing and toys to other missionary children or to African families that could use them. I'm not sure I could have done that as graciously as she did.

None of us had to look very hard to find work to keep us busy, and work was probably our best friend during those days. Somehow we managed to get through Christmas and New Year's Day. By the middle of January, life was starting to get back to normal.

• • •

One day in January, Loren went with the African pastors to their regularly scheduled meeting. They walked because no roads went in that direction. When they were ready to return, Loren told the pastors he was going to walk home by himself a different way because he needed to talk to the Lord about something.

According to Loren, the Lord had been asking him to tell Him thank you for taking John home. Loren didn't want to say something he didn't mean; so he had been arguing with the Lord. But that day as he walked home, he told the Lord "Thank you" because that was what the Lord was asking him to do.

The next day the African pastors started coming to Loren one by one and asking for forgiveness because they had all been thinking that the Lord was partial to white folks because the missionaries never had a child die. Now they were convinced God was not partial. He loved all people just the same. This gave those men a confidence in God they had not had before and brought revival to the African pastors of Jebulungu.

Note: I do not believe God causes the bad things that happen to people, but I believe when bad things happen accidentally or because of the free will of all people, He is so wise and so creative He can bring something good out of even the worst circumstances.

Loren and Lois Clark with their son John, about age 3.

John with a pet dik-dik, the smallest Kenyan antelope.

Hotchkiss Memorial Church at Tenwek. John Clark was buried in the corner between the right wing and the center wing.

Arap Koech teaches John to shoot an arrow.

CHAPTER EIGHT

Kiplang'at

One day in the 1950s I was examining a woman with heart problems who had come to our hospital. She had walked in as our patients usually did, and I marveled that she had made it. But maybe she had learned to go slowly and stop and rest frequently.

As I took her history and did the physical exam, my attention was drawn to the little boy on her lap. He was leaning against her but sitting ramrod straight and not moving at all except for his eyes. His attention was totally centered on me. He followed my every movement. He showed no sign of fear even when I got close and touched him or his mother. He was very thin; even his little cheeks were sunk in. He didn't smile; so I could not tell if he had teeth yet. His hair looked normal – sometimes hair will relax into soft curls if one has been very sick.

When I finished with the mother, I told her we needed to send her to the government hospital in Kericho because we did not have the proper equipment to care for her at Tenwek Hospital. She replied that her husband would come in a few days, and she wanted to stay at our hospital until then.

Then I asked about the boy: "What do we call him?"

"Kiplang'at," she replied. That name meant he had been born in the evening.

"When was he born?"

"Just after we finished planting corn," she said. That meant that he was roughly six months old.

Little Kiplang'at made no protest and showed no fear when an African nurse took him away to be weighed. His weight was 6 ¼ pounds – less than many newborns! He was skin and bones – very little muscle there with which to move. His frame had grown some but probably not as much as it should have in six months. Because he was so thin and the skin pulled so tightly around his skull, his eyes looked bigger than normal for his size.

When I tried to move him, he felt stiff but not the stiffness of tetanus. He had neither the arched back nor the clamped jaw of tetanus. He gave the impression that if one was not careful in the way one handled him, he just might break!

I don't know how much thinking a six-month-old does, and I didn't think of it then, but I'm wondering now if, at times, he had been fed by other mothers who had milk to spare. So maybe at this point, he was watching me closely to see if I would feed him. Probably not. He probably just thought I looked a lot like other people he had seen, but then, at the same time, I looked a lot different than anybody he had ever seen before!

His eyes were not pleading for help. They seemed to portray a solemn stoicism – a stoic acceptance of whatever life handed him.

I admitted both the mother and the child. The mother would be in our big general ward. We diapered little Kiplang'at and put him in a crib in a small room by himself. He did not need to be exposed to a ward full of sick people! And besides, someone was going to be waking him up and feeding him every four hours or so.

That afternoon I read about starvation. I learned that stiffness is a sign of advanced starvation. Without intervention, Kiplang'at at best, only had a few days to live. His mother said he had no trouble swallowing and had no vomiting or diarrhea. But I didn't want to take any chances. So for the first few days, I was going to do the feedings myself. I wanted to know firsthand how he was reacting to food.

I chose a formula with cow's milk as a base because that's what was available and what the family would use later at home.

We kept no milk on hand at the hospital, so I borrowed some from our house. At Freedom Hall we had milk delivered regularly. Our cook strained it to remove any foreign materials such as grit or hair and the occasional tadpole. Tadpoles meant that the milk supply had been a little short, and our supplier had added river water so we would get the full amount.

After straining the milk, our cook boiled it. Boiling changed the flavor only a little, and the milk was still very drinkable. The texture of the cream, however, was changed by boiling. The cream became tough and would not readily mix back into the milk. It could still be whipped and used for cooking or for making butter, and it still tasted good. But for Kiplang'at, cream was out of the question; it would plug up the nipple on the bottle I was going to use to feed him.

Before my evening meal, I gave him his first bottle. I picked him up carefully and held him to feed him. He took the bottle eagerly, but after a bit he stopped and turned away. I tried to get him to take some more, but he would not take the nipple.

I scolded him in English and said in what I hoped was a soothing, comforting voice, "You'll never make it if you won't take more than an ounce-and-a half at a feeding!"

I tried to burp him but got no response. I hugged him gently, tucked him in, prayed for his survival and went to my house for supper.

Before I retired, I went back to the hospital and offered him another bottle. That time he took 3 ounces, and I was encouraged. That time, I got a satisfactory burp!

In the middle of the night, he took another 5 ½ ounces. He was showing no signs of gastric distress or any kind of intolerance to the formula. I don't recall that he had problems with elimination even though little had gone through his system in recent days and maybe for a long time.

By the next day, about 16 hours after he had taken the first three tablespoons of milk, Kiplang'at was taking the full 8 ounces of the formula. On the third day, the sucking muscles in his cheeks were back to normal, and he had fat little cheeks like a baby should have. I wished I had thought to take a picture of him on the day we first saw him. He still had a lot of weight to gain, but his face no longer looked like he was starving. And the stiffness was disappearing; he was beginning to demonstrate the random movements of babyhood.

The father came and agreed his wife should go to the hospital in Kericho. "But Kiplang'at stays here," he said. "I can see he is much better."

Traditionally, Kipsigis men paid little attention to their children until they were about a year old. But this man obviously had taken a good look at his son before the child was brought to Tenwek and another good look after he had been with us for about 3 days. Kiplang'at's father could see his little boy was already improving.

I knew the father cared deeply for Kiplang'at, and I was glad he wanted Kiplang'at to stay with us. I believe the mother cared for Kiplang'at too, but she was so sick herself that she did not realize what was happening to him. Or maybe she did know and came to Tenwek, not for herself, but hoping to get help for Kiplang'at.

On the third or fourth day, feeling the effects of sleep deprivation, I quickly made the formula for one of the feedings and hurried to feed Kiplang'at. He took one swallow and screamed. I thought the formula must have been too hot, but when I checked it, that was not the case. I tried again; again he screamed. He didn't cry; he just gave one piercing scream and looked at me with his big solemn eyes. I sat there thinking, and suddenly I knew: In my haste, I had failed to add the sugar to the formula. I started to laugh and said to him, "Three days ago you were starving, and now you refuse to eat because there is no sugar in your milk?"

Gone was the stoic acceptance of whatever life handed him. This boy was going to be a fighter. That was good, and I was proud of him. He did not cry when I left the room to correct my mistake, and when I returned, he took all of his feeding with no more complaints.

The African nurses' aids gradually took over most of Kiplang'at's care, but he was still my project. In the African nurses, Kiplang'at had about a dozen big sisters and aunties who loved him and looked after him. As he grew older, they took him to their quarters, played with him and fed him. They taught him to speak Kipsigis, to eat gimyet (a thick cornmeal mush) and to drink mursik (sour milk flavored with charcoal.)

If I was working late catching up on paperwork, the girls brought Kiplang'at into the office, and he sat on my lap and watched as I worked. He watched quietly while he played with something that was handy – and safe – and I loved having him there.

The African nurses started calling me "Kobot Kiplang'at." At first it was obviously a tentative statement, said with a smile and a twinkle in the eye, and accompanied by a close observation of my reaction. Would I accept the name or not?

The name roughly meant "Mother of Kiplang'at" but also denoted something special about the child: Usually the Kipsigis people used the title with the first child but sometimes with the name of a favorite child or of one who had accomplished something remarkable. Kiplang'at qualified – he had been close to death and now was making a marvelous recovery.

Because of my love for Kiplang'at, my initial reaction was a big, uncontrollable smile. At the same time, I felt that the Kipsigis people allowing a foreigner, a white American woman, to use a name like that indicated a degree of acceptance into the tribe, and I liked that, too.

They called me Kobot Kiplang'at until one day when some patients who didn't really know me started calling me by that name. The nurses' aides quickly told them, "No, no, no. She's not his mother – but she loves him and takes care of him." After that the nurse's aides used the name only in private conversations.

As I recall, Kiplang'at stayed with us more than 2 years. (He was still there when our doctor came in 1959.) Then one day Kiplang'at's father came and told us he would be back on the following week to pick up Kiplang'at and take him home. Seeing him go was hard, and

I prayed that the Lord would help him adjust quickly to life in an African hut.

A few months later the father brought Kiplang'at in for some minor problem. That was the last time I ever saw him. Soon I left to come back to the States. I did not return to Kenya, but I carried a picture of Kiplang'at in my wallet for years. Then the only reason I didn't have it was because I failed to transfer the picture to my new wallet.

Although I was not Kiplang'at's mother, I was the person who, with the Lord's help, gave him back his life. Almost anyone could have done that for Kiplang'at, but I was the one who was in the right place at the right time, and I am forever thankful for that. God gave me an important role in his life for a short time.

Kiplang'at influenced my life as well; in a very subtle way, he changed my identity, and that change has been permanent. No matter how old I get, no matter where I live, no matter what language surrounds me, I know in my heart that I am and always will be "Kobot Kiplang'at," mother of Kiplang'at.

Kiplang'at shortly before he went to live with his father.

Kiplang'at and Thomas. Both of these children were in our care.

Millie and Kiplang'at when he was about a year old.

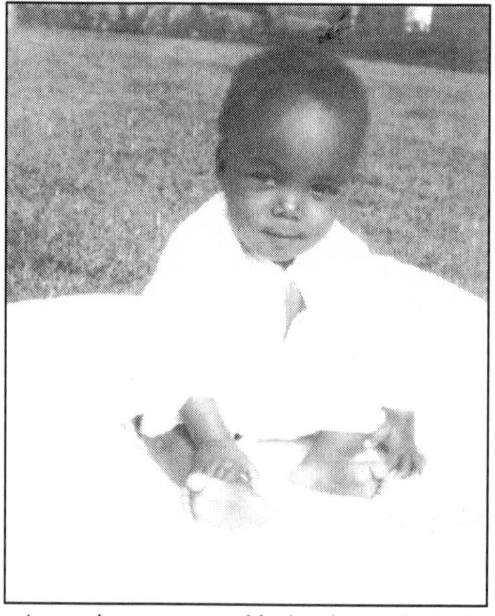

Kiplang'at at about one year old when he weighed 14 pounds.

CHAPTER NINE
Did that really happen?

Smallpox was always around in the Highlands of Kenya during the 1950s. We saw no cases at the hospital because those who had smallpox were not very sick and needed no medical attention. But during my second term in the late 1950s, I had the unique experience of seeing a smallpox case from start to finish.

One evening as I was eating supper, one of the African nurses' aides came to the back door to tell me a patient who had delivered a good-sized baby boy that day had developed a rash. I told her I would be up as soon as I finished eating. As she turned to go, she added almost apologetically, "I don't know if it's smallpox."

Why would she suspect smallpox because of a rash? I wondered as I finished eating and took part in the conversation around the table.

About a half hour later, I examined the woman in question. The rash had disappeared, and she was feeling fine. But she had had a rash; the nurses' aide had seen it and reported it. I decided we had better move this woman and her baby to a more private room. We had no place to isolate her because none of our rooms had bathrooms, cooking facilities, or running water.

The African girls helped the mother and baby move and get settled in their new quarters. I went to the office and read up on smallpox. Sure enough, smallpox is usually preceded by a transient rash a couple of days before the smallpox lesions start to appear. The rash is usually on the forehead or over the stomach. How did my young nurses' aide know this, and I didn't? I asked myself, thankful she had mentioned it and probably steered me in the right direction. Sometime later I realized she had grown up with smallpox all around her and probably had heard the women talk about the rash that comes and goes and is a sign of the sickness that will follow in a few days.

A couple of days later, the patient began showing signs of emerging lesions all over her body. They were just little bumps under her skin, but each one felt as if buckshot were in it. For three days in her chart, I described the lesions and then added, "Doesn't look like smallpox."

But on the fourth or fifth day, the lesions began to fit the textbook description of smallpox. They had the "pearly" appearance that is peculiar to smallpox. This new mother's body was covered with pox. She even had a few lesions on the palms of her hands and on the soles of her feet! I charted: "Looks like smallpox."

Oddly, at the same time I was watching the OB patient for confirmation of smallpox, a boy of about 11 in the general ward (in with some kidney problems, as I remember) also broke out with smallpox. He had a light case, typical of the smallpox common in our area, and his symptoms were a day or two ahead of the woman's.

At the end of each month, we had to send a tally of all the medical problems we had seen that month to the English Medical Officer stationed in Kericho. So that month I added two cases of smallpox. This alarmed the Medical Officer, and he called on the phone to inquire about them. Upon hearing that one of them was a severe case, he decided to come and see for himself.

On the day he arrived, I met him in the residential area, and we walked up to the hospital together. We came to the little boy first. The doctor stood back, looked at the boy and said, "Hmm, Variola Minor," emphasizing the word minor.

We went on to see the new mother. As we came around the corner of the building, there she was with her baby, sitting on a blanket in the sunshine. When the doctor saw her, he stopped and stared. "Hmm," he said, nodding his head, "Variola Major."

Then he turned his attention to me. "Now we've had smallpox in this area for 25 years," he said, "and we haven't had a death. And we don't want a death now. You see that she doesn't die."

I suggested that maybe he should take her and the baby back to Kericho with him, but he said, "No, no. She'll do just fine here." He did suggest that we dust her with sulfa powder twice a day to prevent any infection in the pox. We did that, and she sat around looking like a ghost! But she didn't get infected.

Yes, if you're wondering, the baby got smallpox. After the normal incubation period, he broke out with nine spots. He wasn't even fussy, and he got a permanent immunity to smallpox from it. One more smallpox case to report!

After the pox had dried up and there was no more danger of infection, the mother and child went home, and we did not see them again. I hope they had long and happy lives.

No one else that I know of got smallpox as a result of our three cases in the hospital. And I felt blessed I had been able to watch the development of a smallpox case from the precursory rash to the drying up of the pox because smallpox was soon to be extinct.

About 20 years later, the last few cases of smallpox anywhere in the world were recorded, and no one has experienced it or seen it since.

• • •

During my time in Kenya, I delivered one set of triplets. Edna Boraff, who spent years in charge of the maternity ward at Tenwek, delivered 15 sets or more, but she worked at it over a longer period of time than I did. At Tenwek we had a higher percentage of twins and triplets than one would expect to see in America. That was because every mother did not deliver at the hospital. If labor was uncomplicated, the mother delivered at home, unassisted, or sometimes on the path as she was coming to the hospital. In that case, the mother turned around and took her newborn back home.

If a woman was pregnant with more than one baby, she tended to have more complications, and so more women with twins or triplets came to the hospital. Complications included premature babies, delay in the birth of the second or third baby, and babies being positioned in such a way that they were unable to enter the birth canal.

Our patient walked in as most of the patients did. She was in labor, and she told us she was having twins. A few hours later she delivered a well-developed little boy who weighed a little over 5 ½ pounds.

Soon she delivered the placenta and then the contractions stopped. Her uterus was firm, the bleeding was controlled, and the remaining baby's heart beat was good. No unusual activity by the unborn baby indicated any problems such as a lack of oxygen.

I have been trying to remember why we didn't send the mother to Kericho to be seen by a doctor. But we didn't, we must have had a good reason. It could possibly be because her condition was not an emergency, we were too busy, or the trip would have been a hardship for her.

A couple days later, her labor started again, and, in due time the mother delivered identical twin girls, each weighing more than 5 ½ pounds. This meant that the mother was carrying more than 17 pounds of babies plus two placentas and an enlarged uterus to hold all that. She must have been a big woman, but I do not remember her looking overly large or out of proportion when I first saw her before she delivered the boy.

The Kipsigis believed that in the case of triplets, the middle child is not a person but an animal, and so the second child is killed as soon as it is born before it starts to breathe.

This mother did not seem alarmed that she had three babies. Times were changing, and maybe she had accepted the new idea that all three babies were, in fact, people. Or possibly she did not consider her three to be triplets – after all the boy was a single birth, and a couple days later the twins were born! Anyway, a few days later, she went home happily with all three.

African babies are not born black; they are dusky at birth and darken noticeably in the first few days. So the little boy was dark by the time the girls were born, and they looked light by comparison. They looked as if they came from separate families – maybe even from separate races.

I'm thankful I got to deliver that one set of triplets. As I have thought of them from time to time through the years, I've wondered what has happened to them and what their lives were like. And I've wondered how the mother coped with three infants, then with three toddlers, and later with three teenagers!

CHAPTER TEN
Freedom Hall

Freedom Hall was the name of the single ladies' house at Tenwek when I lived there in the 1950s. The house consisted of five bedrooms, a kitchen, a pantry, a living room, a dining room, a storage room, an office, and a shed and an outhouse out back. During my time there, we never had more than five single ladies at a time, so the building was big enough. Later, as hospital staffing increased, too many single ladies were at Tenwek; so the mission built apartments, and each single lady had her own apartment.

I'm glad I got to live in Freedom Hall. I liked the company of the others, and I learned a lot from them, especially during the first few years I was there.

The occupancy of our house changed frequently. Someone would be packing up, putting her things in storage, and leaving for furlough in America. And soon, someone else would be coming to be part of our household for four or five years.

Once we knew the language fairly well, we each took a turn (a month at a time) running the household. We had a cook and two houseboys to do the work. We had to see they had the supplies they needed and they did the work right. We told the cook what to fix, but if something didn't need to be cooked, we fixed that ourselves.

Tenwek had a small generator; so we had electricity every evening from 6:00 to 10:00. If you wanted to stay up later for any reason, you lit candles, lamps or lanterns. The hospital paid for the generator to run three mornings a week so they could do hospital laundry. Because electricity was available during those times, anybody else could use it as well. We could not depend on anything that required around-the-clock electricity. So the missionaries and the hospital did without a lot of things that were routine in America. I think every house had a kerosene refrigerator, and they served us well.

We had a lot of fun at Freedom Hall. Sometimes we did things the married couples never thought of doing, such as going down to the river and eating lunch or dinner there. We took one of the boys with us to help a little but mostly to be able to answer questions and stop rumors that might get started again. Long before I got to Tenwek, the rumor was circulating that the Americans went down to the river to eat because they didn't want other people to see what they were eating – things such as lizards!

We had breakfast at 7:00 a.m., lunch at noon and dinner (or supper) at 6:00 p.m. And because we were in an English colony, we had tea at 10:00 a.m. and 4:00 p.m. That way, if English company dropped in about tea time, we could easily invite them to stay for tea. We knew the boys were already planning it for 10:00 a.m. and 4:00 p.m.

I remember when I first arrived in Kenya, I was always hungry. I still don't know what made me so hungry. But at tea-time when most people ate one or two cookies, I usually ate six! That seemed to go on forever, but I eventually got over it.

Usually the nurses had morning tea at the hospital with the African nurses. It was good for all of us to be together at least once a day to visit and get to know one another. Also it was a good time for announcements, etc. Of course, at times medical procedures took precedence over tea-time, and in that case, we grabbed a cup of tea whenever and wherever we could.

The single ladies usually took afternoon tea in Freedom Hall. If you needed to see one of the other missionaries about anything, this was a good time to go to his or her house to talk. I think that during much of my second term when I was the only nurse at Tenwek, I seldom went to the house for afternoon tea.

• • •

One time reports were coming in that a big snake was down by the river above the falls. The people were saying this snake was about 300 years old (we never did find out what brought them to that conclusion). So one afternoon, Eva and I went down to see if we could locate the creature. We were walking along slowly and watchfully when I saw it about 20 feet ahead, sunning itself on a big flat rock.

"There it is," I whispered.

The next thing I knew, Eva, probably the bravest girl in our house, was crouched behind me, peering around my left shoulder, whispering, "Where?"

I pointed, and when she had located the snake, she stood beside me again. She just needed to know where it was. We probably watched from that vantage point for about 15 minutes.

The snake's head was beautifully colored, mostly a bright green. The head was about the size of a man's clenched fist; the body was correspondingly large. We could see only four or five feet of the body; vegetation hid the rest. And we were not in a position to see any sort of pattern or design on the snake's back. However, we could easily tell this was a constrictor.

The snake was aware of our presence and constantly shot out its tongue to gather information about us.

When we got back to Tenwek, we told the men, and immediately a group of African and American men armed with guns and knives went down to kill it because it was in an area of the river where the women washed clothes and frequently brought small children with them. The snake would have been a real threat to the children. But the snake had moved away from the big rock, and they did not find it. No one saw the snake again in our area; apparently it had moved on to a more private spot.

• • •

Betty was one of the single ladies. She had grown up in Kenya – living three months of every year at Tenwek with her missionary family and nine months of every year at Rift Valley Academy. When her family was in the States on furlough, they lived in town, so Betty never had any farm experience that most youngsters got during and before the 1950s.

One evening at the supper table Betty announced happily, "You know that little white goat of Tapkigen's? Well, she had a calf!" The other three of us at the table burst into uproarious laughter, and Betty looked confused.

In my mind I could see one of my Dad's long-legged, tall Holstein calves looking down quizzically at Tapkigen's little white goat and questioning "Mama?" We were all laughing so hard that none of us could explain to Betty why we were laughing. But she finally figured it out and said, "Well, a goatlet then!"

More laughter. Finally Eva got enough control to say, "It's a kid." That didn't help; Betty was still confused. But when Eva added, "A baby goat is a kid," Betty understood.

• • •

When Eva was in charge of the household, she frequently made a dessert that was one of our favorites. It was a moist, dark cake with dates and nuts, and she usually topped it with whipped cream. One evening as we were being served this delicious concoction, one of the ladies asked her what she called it. Without hesitation Eva said, "Old Maid's Delight." And all us old maids around the table burst into laughter.

From that evening on, whenever we had company and that dessert, someone was sure to let our company know they were eating

Old Maid's Delight. I guess we were all so busy and so happy that we didn't mind calling ourselves old maids.

I often wondered if Eva's answer was as spontaneous as it looked or if she had already decided on the name and was just waiting for someone to ask the right question.

However, several months later, as I was looking at my dessert and waiting for the others to be served, I had a spontaneous thought and I casually asked, "Do you think this is called Old Maid's Delight because it's a date with a nut?" Once again, all the old maids laughed, and the story to be shared with our guests became just a little longer.

Millie Roseman (left) and Betty Adkins in front of Freedom Hall.

Buying eggs at Freedom Hall. The house boy submerged the eggs in cool water. If they stayed on their sides, we bought them; if they stood or floated, we did not buy them.

All five of the single missionary ladies in front of the poinsettia bush: Alice Day, Maisie Doyle, Edna Boroff, Millie Roseman and Amy Hauvermail.

CHAPTER ELEVEN
Ernest and Ludiah

One evening at the supper table, Eva, one of my housemates, said to me, "Millie, Ludiah looks like she could have her baby any time now, and when she does, I want to know right away. Shoot off the cannon – once if it's a boy and twice if it's a girl!"

"Okay," I said wondering how I could improvise a cannon shot.

Ludiah was a teacher at the secondary school where Eva was the principal. When I first met Ludiah, she was in the Girl's Boarding School just a short distance down the hill from our house. Her father was a chief, and even as a school girl, Ludiah showed traits of leadership. She was a devoted Christian. She was tall and large boned and evoked thoughts of a strong, hard-working Kipsigis wife.

But Ludiah had other plans. When she finished secondary school, she went on to Teacher Training at a school outside of the tribal area. And when she was a qualified teacher, she returned to Tenwek and got a job teaching at the secondary school.

Sometime during her growing-up years, Ludiah met Ernest, another Kipsigis teacher, also a Christian, and they fell in love. Ludiah's father disliked Ernest and kept trying to arrange a marriage with someone else for Ludiah. But each time, Ludiah said she did not want to marry that one – she wanted to marry Ernest. And in the end, the father agreed to let them marry.

Ludiah's father and Ernest settled on a bride price (usually 4 or more cows). Ernest gave Ludiah's father the specified number of cows, and Ernest and Ludiah were married.

Ernest had built a house for them near the secondary school so Ludiah could easily walk to work. He taught in one of our outlying primary schools and rode his bicycle to and from his school.

I never saw their house but imagine it was not the typical Kipsigis dwelling. Some of the young men were starting to build larger homes with several rooms and the kitchen outside in another small shelter or a lean-to. Although still mud and wattle buildings, these homes were rectangular and even had a window or two and a hinged door. This is the kind of house I think Ernest would have built for Ludiah.

Because Ludiah was working full time, Ernest helped her plant their first garden. Traditionally, the garden that supplied food for the family was women's work from the preparation of the ground (a shallow hoeing with a heavy, cumbersome-looking hoe) to constant weeding, to harvest. Cash crops, a new possibility for income, were the man's responsibility.

Ludiah had taken classes in cooking and nutrition and had learned about many more vegetables than those found in the typical Kipsigis garden that she could use in meal preparation. So when she and Ernest planted their first garden, she planted things Ernest didn't recognize. He asked her if she knew what to do with them after they were grown. She laughed and assured him she knew how to cook them. Ludiah's garden was different from the gardens of the other Kipsigis wives.

Eva had told me that Ludiah and Ernest had bought a crib and already had set it up in their home. That meant that the baby would not be sleeping with the mother. So I fixed a box with bedding in it to be on the stand beside Ludiah's bed in the OB ward. This baby would get used to sleeping alone from the very beginning.

On some heavy paper I drew two very simple cannons. One or both of them would be delivered by hand to Eva to let her know the baby had arrived and whether it was a boy or a girl.

I took both the box and the cannons to the OB ward to wait for Ludiah's expected arrival.

A week or so passed before Ludiah put in an appearance, but there she was one morning, waiting with others to be seen. She was in labor and progressing nicely. We put her in the delivery room, and one or two of the African nurses stayed with her.

All morning I was busy seeing other patients and running back and forth to the delivery room to check on Ludiah. By mid-afternoon we had a beautiful, good-sized baby girl.

Everything had gone well – except for one thing. The uterus, the baby's home for nine months, was supposed to contract one last time and stay contracted. When tightened, the uterine muscles pinch the ends of the many blood vessels that have grown to transfer nutrients from the mother to the baby. These blood vessels are no longer needed, but if they are left open, the mother will slowly bleed to death.

When I put my hand on Ludiah's abdomen, I could feel the uterus. It was too big and too soft. When I massaged the uterus, it would contract and become hard, but soon, it was relaxed and soft again. I wanted so much to send my little cannons to Eva (two if it's a girl), but I did not want to send them until I knew Ludiah was totally out of danger.

"Oh Lord, we can't lose Ludiah," I prayed silently as I worked. "She's too important to all of us – especially to Ernest, to the new baby and to Eva; she's important to the whole tribe! Please stop the bleeding."

After a couple of shots and much massaging, I had done everything I knew to do. Everything, that is, except turn my patient over to a doctor. But all the doctors were too far away.

At last I thought, "Forget the cannon! We need help!" I sent one of the African nurses to the residential area to ask the other missionaries to pray that the bleeding would stop. And before the nurse even got to tell anyone, Ludiah's uterus contracted and stayed contracted!

I thought of the verse in Isaiah that says, "Before they call, I will answer." We were all thankful for the Lord's intervention and Ludiah's healing.

Needless to say, we kept a close watch on Ludiah for the next day or so. She had no further problems, for which we were all very thankful.

A couple of days after the baby was born, I walked into the OB ward and was surprised to see Ernest and another young man, a friend of Ernest, standing by Ludiah's bed looking at the baby. The expressions on their faces said volumes about how they were feeling. What an awesome thing to see a perfectly formed little baby and to know that the life in that little body has great capacity to learn and an unknown potential to create and accomplish! And all those insights created an instant love for the baby.

Ludiah was lying on the bed, looking up at the ceiling with an angelic smile on her face. Her expression said that she was translating the expression on her husband's face into a big thank you for a beautiful daughter and a job well done. And she had every right to feel that way.

Because the Kipsigis men were taught to have nothing to do with the birth of a baby and to pay very little attention to their children until they were about a year old, I had not seen the joy and pride of new fathers in Africa as I had seen it in America or England. And for me it was a case of instant homesickness. I wanted to go back to America where the men obviously cared about their wives, and they weren't afraid to show a little emotion when viewing a newborn baby.

Ludiah made a quick recovery from childbirth as the Kipsigis women usually did. She was the only Kipsigis mother I put on a feeding schedule for her baby. Because she was going to be teaching again soon, she needed the baby to eat at specified times and not to expect to be fed on demand. This seemed to work well for them.

A little more than a year after Ludiah's baby was born, I came back to the States ill and did not return to Kenya. But I heard about Ludiah and Ernest from the other missionaries whom I saw when they were home on leave.

While I was in Africa, Kenya was still an English colony. Kenya had an Englishman for a governor, and many of the people in authority were from England. The days of Colonialism were drawing to an end. And the colonies were again to be given the right of self-government. The English authorities did a good job preparing the Kenyans for independence by giving qualified Africans positions of authority such as Assistant Minister of Lands, Assistant Minister of Education, Assistant Minister of Health, etc. So when Kenya got its independence in 1963, the Africans were well-prepared to run a modern government.

Another factor that helped to make a smooth transition was the size of the country and the number of tribes within its borders. Some 30 tribes live in Kenya; the possibility of any one tribe becoming dominate and becoming the ruling class was unlikely. In African countries where only 2 or 3 tribes lived at the time of independence, the tribes showed much jealousy, resulting in bloodshed and a very difficult time for the Africans.

Just after Kenya got its independence in 1963, Ernest somehow got the attention of the authorities in Nairobi, and he was offered the position of Ambassador to Russia. They reasoned that he would do well there "because the Communists could not contaminate his mind." Ernest, Ludiah and family were in Russia for several years.

Later, we heard Ernest and Ludiah were in New York City to meet, orient and encourage Kenyans coming to the States for whatever reason. Ernest and Ludiah served their country well.

Ernest saved his money and bought land in the Highlands of Kenya as it became available, and in the end he had a large coffee plantation.

Oh yes, Ludiah went on to have a family of nine girls!

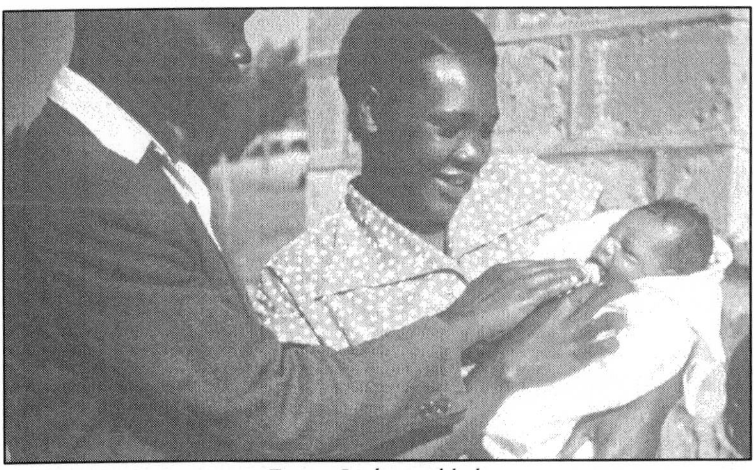

Ernest, Ludea and baby

CHAPTER TWELVE
Animal Encounters

During my time in Kenya, I saw a wide variety of wildlife, from soldier ants to beautiful birds, to elephants. In the Highlands where we lived, we saw none of the large herds of antelope, zebra and wildebeests that were ever-present at the lower elevations. And because they were not present, the carnivores were also not present.

However, a couple of stories came out of the 1930s that made me aware that predators did come into our area occasionally. One time a teenager was attacked by a leopard. The boy killed the leopard and survived but was left with a severely damaged knee.

The second story was about a dog one of our teachers owned. He was a big dog named Samson. At night Samson was chained up behind the teacher's home. One night the teacher heard a frantic scratching at the back door and opened it to find a trembling Samson there with a broken chain. She brought him in the house for the night, and the next morning the missionaries found evidence of a lion's presence. These two incidents took place at or near Tenwek, about 25 miles from the border of the game reserve.

Occasionally we heard of elephants that had come out of the reserve onto the nearby Kipsigis farms. If the millet crop was about half ripe and the elephants ate it, the unripe grain fermented in their stomachs and the elephants were soon drunk. Drunk elephants are unpredictable and dangerous. Kenyan police and/or soldiers were usually called in to kill them.

During my first term in Kenya, someone spotted a python at one of the little farms across the river from Tenwek. It had eaten one of the families' goats. The men of the area banded together, found the python and killed it.

About two weeks after I arrived at Tenwek, Carl and Mary Waggoner asked me to go on a safari with them into the Masai Reserve. The Masai lived there, but the area was really a game reserve. I think we stayed a couple of nights. We slept in tents and sleeping bags and cooked our food over a campfire. Waggoners took two of their houseboys with us.

The first night we retired early to get ready for a big day of touring the reserve and watching the animals. I woke up in the middle of the night, opened the tent door and looked outside. The fire was almost out. Suddenly I heard the tramping of some heavy animal close to our camp. Quickly I crawled back into my sleeping bag.

Soon I heard Carl talking to the Africans. I stuck my head out again to ask what was happening. He said a large animal was close by, and he was asking the boys to build up the fire again to keep whatever it was away. After a good fire was going, I felt safer and went back to sleep.

When I woke up in the morning, I was perspiring. Maybe the sleeping bag was a bit heavy for an African night, but I had a feeling the perspiration was really a response to the fear that I had felt earlier.

We ate breakfast, packed up our equipment and were on our way. Very close to where we had camped, we saw a lone rhino feeding in a grassy area. He was probably our nocturnal visitor.

When I got back to Tenwek, I read some material on rhinos. Among other things, I found out that a lone rhino is usually an old male, very irritable and dangerous. I was thankful for a safe and happy safari.

• • •

During my time in Kenya, I had two pets – a border collie named Mickey and a small monkey named Bobo.

Mickey was my first pet there and the first dog I ever had as my own. Most of the time he stayed close to our house and slept in my room. Some nights he accompanied our night watchman on his rounds. I never took Mickey to the hospital.

I enjoyed Mickey, but I have only two specific memories of our time together. One day I was really upset about something. (What it was is not even a vague memory now.) I went into our house crying, ran up the stairs into my room and threw myself on the bed. Immediately Mickey was by my side, although he knew he was not allowed on the bed. He got close to my face and looked at me expectantly as much as to say, "Just tell me what's wrong, and I'll fix it." His love and concern for me touched my heart. I reached out and pulled him close. We lay there together until we both felt better and could get on with our responsibilities.

Mickey helped me that day, but sometime later, I had a chance to help him. One evening when I came down from the hospital, Mickey was in our backyard frantically biting at his skin. A brief examination disclosed the cause – soldier ants!! The sun was setting, and the fire had been started in our fireplace. So I spread a white sheet in front of the fireplace and got Mickey to stand or sit on that sheet. As the ants dropped off of him, I killed them (probably with a fly swatter) and threw them in the fire.

In my second term, my pet was Bobo, a little monkey some African children had captured in a cornfield. They brought him to the Bible School property where a retired builder and his wife were living and supervising the construction of the buildings needed for the Bible School. I suppose they gave the children a few coins or some cookies for Bobo. I think he was young enough to drink from a bottle when they first got him. By the time I got him, he had graduated to fruit and vegetables. When the couple went home on leave, they gave Bobo to me.

Bobo was lots of fun – and a little bit of work, too. He wasn't housebroken, so I had to diaper him. He didn't like being diapered and kept trying to pull the diaper off. When you consider that he had two hands, two feet and a tail, and I had only 2 hands, you can imagine this task took extra time and effort so he couldn't pull the diaper off. (The diaper had a small hole in it for the tail.)

Bobo was like a young human in many ways – he had a security blanket, and he did not like it when anyone took that away from him. He felt safe around people he knew but was uncertain about strangers.

One day I took Bobo with me when I went to the African nurse's home for something. The girls were mostly teenagers and were intrigued by Bobo. Finally one of the girls gently pulled Bobo's blanket away from him and dropped it about six feet from where I was standing. He chattered at her and kept looking from me to his blanket. I think he really wanted me to help him get the blanket back. He finally jumped down to the floor and made several false starts before getting up enough courage to go the six feet to retrieve his blanket. When he had it, he came racing back to me and back into my arms. He turned around, looked at the girls and chattered at them some more.

I was proud of my little monkey for working up the courage to get his blanket back, and I was proud of my nurses for not scaring Bobo or hindering him from doing what he felt he needed to do.

I'm glad I had Mickey and Bobo for pets. They helped me to relax and gave me a break from the pressures of the hospital.

I left both of these animals in Kenya when I came home; I gave them to other missionaries, and I never heard what finally happened with either one.

• • •

On one of my trips to the coast for some R and R, I took a leisurely walk by myself. The tide was going out, so when I came to a rocky outcropping, I walked around to see what was on the other side. The beach was empty; no other person was in sight. I stood looking up at the vegetation on the hill that rose abruptly from the sandy beach and wondered what it would have been like to have been an early explorer shipwrecked on a beach like this one.

Suddenly I saw movement above the vegetation – the heads and necks of two hooded cobras! They were interacting in some way – fighting? playing? courting? I didn't know. I knew some cobras spit at their enemies, aiming for the eyes and are very accurate at twenty feet or closer. I was probably about twenty feet from them. I quickly left, going around the outcropping of rocks and headed back to where I was staying.

A couple of African men, resort employees, were coming toward me. I told them I had seen two snakes on the other side of the rocks. They asked me to show them, so I went back around the rocks with them, and pointed to the hillside. The snakes were gone. Not knowing where they were made me uncomfortable, and I quickly took my leave and went back around the rocks.

Later I read that some cobras can move as fast as forty miles an hour. I was glad they hadn't come after me!

• • •

A couple of weeks before I came home, I went on my last safari in the game reserve. Many things about this safari are unclear in my mind. A few other things are forever burned in my memory. I don't know what time of day we left Tenwek, I don't remember how many nights we were out there, and I can't even tell you who exactly went on that safari. So, some of these incidents will be prefaced by "I think" or "probably."

I think we left Tenwek early, got into the game reserve, located a good camping spot, set up our tents and started a fire. Then some of us went looking for water. After much searching, the only water we found was in a muddy watering hole. Gene Lewton had brought a five-gallon milk can for the water, and Ernie, the doctor, must have OK'd filling that can with the water we found.

Back at camp, we set the can on three stones over the fire and left it to heat. And then the men went hunting.

After the water boiled, we periodically skimmed the trash off the top and threw it away. Meanwhile we read, played games, worked a jigsaw puzzle, or just waited for the men to come back. We wanted to see if we would have any meat to add to our brown water.

The men probably returned to camp around 4 p.m., a couple of hours before sunset. One of them had killed an impala, a large antelope. They had dressed it and partially skinned it before loading it into the pickup. As soon as they returned, they gave the cooks enough meat for the evening meal. The Africans already had potatoes, carrots and onions ready to add to the pot.

The men finished skinning the animal, and then the hunters tied a rope around the carcass, threw the end of the rope over a high branch of a tree and pulled the carcass up in to the tree. This prevented predators from getting to the meat, and it allowed the meat to air-dry on the outside and prevent the moist meat inside from spoiling.

After we ate, the night was dark, and we sat around the campfire singing and talking. The scent of the kill was in the air, and we could hear at least one lion roaring at intervals as he got closer and closer to our camp. Finally we all decided to retire to our tents. The Africans built up the fire again before retiring.

I was sharing a tent with Lewton's young son, Kenny, about 7 years old. Our sleeping bags were on tarps on the ground. After Kenny was tucked in, I tied our tent door shut, crawled into my sleeping bag and blew out my lantern. Sleep did not come easily, and I woke up frequently during the night. Once I heard something drinking from my wash basin, which was just outside our tent door.

Every time I woke up, I pulled my pillow about three inches farther down into the sleeping bag. The last time I woke up, daylight had come, and I found myself curled in the bottom of my bag with my pillow about halfway down the sleeping bag.

Kenny had a dream that night. He said that he had heard a noise behind our tent and went out to see what it was, and Auntie Millie was out there kissing a giraffe!

The next day two Masai men came by and asked if we had found good water. When they heard we hadn't, they offered to show us where to get some. I went with the group to see the good water. A small ravine with several trees growing out of it was near our camp. They led us down into that rock-walled ravine. A small stream about a foot across and six inches deep of clear water ran over the rocky floor at the bottom. We followed the men for what seemed a long walk. Many places were so narrow we had to walk single file.

My imagination became active, and I wondered if a leopard was just beyond us at the water source. If he saw all these people, he would feel trapped and try to fight his way out. I was glad the Masai leading us both carried spears. As soon as I satisfactorily settled the possibility of a leopard in my mind, I wondered if a thirsty python lay somewhere along the ravine wall....

At last we came to a small spring of clear, cool water. The water shot out of a hole in the rock wall with enough pressure behind it to let it drop away from the wall and into the headwaters of the little stream. We easily filled our containers and returned to camp happy that for the rest of our stay we would have good water. We were thankful to the Masai for sharing one of their precious resources with us.

As you can see, living in a tribal area adjacent to a wildlife preserve had its perks. None of us regularly took days off, and Sundays were always busy. So it was good to be able to take two or three days every few months to relax and enjoy God's creations. The men who liked to hunt got hunting permits easily, so this was also a source of fresh meat for us.

Ever since my youth I have been impressed with the diversity of God's creation – not only did He make the animals different but he also made them to eat different foods. Then He had to make a different digestive system for each species. Then He somehow had to instill instincts in each kind of animal so they would know just what to eat. With these few words I am just scratching the surface of the wisdom God used to create all of the animal life we might encounter if we could explore the whole world.

Then God created mankind. Man is part of the animal kingdom – but not just the top of the food chain. According to God, man was created in the image of God. From Adam on, that image has been marred by sin. God knew even as He was still creating that sin would separate mankind from Him, and so, from the very beginning, He had a plan to bring mankind back to Himself. God's plan was to send His Son to live on earth for 33 years without sinning and then to experience death for the sins of all mankind so all who believed in Jesus would have eternal life (see John 3:16).

I have experienced that salvation and want to tell you it is the greatest blessing that anyone of our species could ever experience.

Masai herdboy

Masai warriors and herdboys visiting our camp. The Masai men and herdboys always carried their spears with them because many predators lived in their area.

A lion with a kill.

A Masai village

Mickey, Millie's border collie.

CHAPTER THIRTEEN
Johanna Arap Ng'etich

Shortly after I arrived in Kenya, I was introduced to the three African elders of our church in the Kipsigis tribe: Zephaniah, Dishon and Johanna. Zephaniah must have lived the farthest from Tenwek. I saw him infrequently and did not get to know him very well. He was a big man, tall and heavy set. He was usually surrounded by other Kipsigis men, and I know he cared much for his people.

Dishon, too, was a big man. He had a warm and friendly personality and was a great leader. Dishon is a Biblical name. I have seen it a few times in the lists of names in the Old Testament. My theory is that our Dishon saw the name, liked the sound of it and consequently chose it as his Christian name. The Kipsigis Christians customarily take a "Christian" name when they are baptized. Usually it is a Biblical name but can be any name they like.

When Dishon was a young man, one evening as he was walking home, a leopard that had wandered into the area attacked him. The leopard bit hard on his knee and would not let go. In the ensuing fight, Dishon was able to kill the leopard and then get himself home. No medical help was available. His parents did the best they could, and eventually the wounds healed. But because his knee healed in a permanently bent position, walking on that leg was impossible. He became able to get around slowly with the help of a walking stick.

Years later, someone suggested he seek medical help. I think he must have gone to Nairobi for the surgery. The doctors straightened the leg, making walking on it possible, even though the joint was now stiff in the straight position. Dishon always had a distinct walk but could make good time on that repaired leg.

Dishon endeared himself to me one afternoon about four years after I first met him. Hazel, the missionary teacher at Cheptenye, and I had been to Nairobi for some reason and came back on the taxi. The "tagis" as it was called was really a small bus that transported mostly Africans. Our baggage was put on top of the taxi with crates of chickens, bags of cabbages and other assorted belongings. When we got to Kericho, Dishon was there to meet someone else. He was surprised to see us and greeted us enthusiastically. Soon someone among the onlookers said, "Who are these old women?" (Don't worry. That was a term of respect!)

Dishon laughed. "Oh these," he said as he motioned to identify the two of us. "These are our children." And by saying that he partially fulfilled Matthew 19:29 for me and made both Hazel and me feel like we really belonged. Matthew 19:29 says: "And everyone who has left houses or brothers or sisters or father or mother or wife or children or lands for My name's sake shall receive a hundred fold, and inherit eternal life." Dishon went on to explain that one of us was a teacher and one was a nurse, and we worked at Cheptenye.

Johanna, the third elder, lived across the river from Tenwek; so we saw him a lot. Many stories circulated about Johanna. I heard from the missionary men that Johanna could out walk any of them when they went out together to tell their neighbors about Jesus. This was surprising because he appeared to be old, and he was short and small-boned. I also heard that he and his wife had adopted 3 children –an uncommon thing among the Kipsigis.

Johanna had served as gun bearer for Karamoja Bell, a Scottish white hunter in Kenya in the early 1900s. I never heard how old Johanna was when he took that job but have always thought of him as a young teenager. His name was not Johanna then, and, because I do not know his childhood name, I'm going to refer to him in this incident as the little gun bearer.

One time the hunters were looking for a rogue elephant that was destroying gardens, huts and even people. They had been following the elephant and knew they were close. One morning as they were going out to track the elephant again, they assigned the little gun bearer to stay in camp and take care of things while the rest were gone.

The hunters left and quickly picked up the trail. The rogue had been just a short walk from their camp during the night. The hunting party had been gone for less than an hour when they heard a gunshot from the direction of camp. So they stopped tracking and ran as fast as they could back to the camp.

When they arrived, the big elephant lay in a heap in the center of the camp. But the little gun bearer and the big gun were nowhere to be seen. The hunters called his name repeatedly but got no answer. Their biggest fear was that the little gun bearer was under the elephant. After making sure the elephant was really dead, a group of hunters worked slowly around the elephant, lifting any skin or body parts they could, looking for the boy, his clothing, or the gun. As they were looking and hoping they wouldn't find anything, a call came from the outskirts of the camp, "Here's the gun!"

Now they had the big gun (and it had been fired) but still no boy. The hunters began searching in the area where the gun was found, and before long, they found the unconscious boy in some bushes 6 to 8 feet from where he had dropped the gun. The big gun had kicked him so hard it knocked him out and sent him flying into the bushes!

Johanna recovered and, according to what I heard, he also became an elephant hunter.

Sometime in his teens he went through the circumcision ceremony and took his adult name of Arap Ng'etich. These ceremonies are a Kipsigis practice and marked the passage from childhood to adulthood.

Also during that time, or maybe a little later, he spent time with Dr. Willis Hotchkiss, the founder of the mission to the Kipsigis, and Arap Ng'etich accepted Jesus as his Savior. Later, he was baptized and took the name of Johanna or John.

I'm not sure if Johanna still worked for Karamoja Bell after his conversion or not. I know that a short time after his conversion, he felt the Lord asking him to go back to his own tribe and tell them about Jesus.

One day a group of us, Africans and missionaries, were going someplace, all riding on the back of a big flatbed truck. Johanna pointed out a big tree in an open area off in the distance and told me that was where he preached his first sermon. He had decided to return to the Kipsigis area and was working his way back to his parents' home, when he came upon a group of Kipsigis who had met to barter goods and services. He had a ready-made audience; so he preached to them!

After Johanna came home, he got married. Time passed, and because his wife did not get pregnant, Johanna did what was customary in Kipsigis. He invited his best friend to sleep with his wife. Soon she was pregnant, but she and the baby both died in childbirth.

When Johanna remarried, he did not try the old custom again. He prayed, and the Lord gave Johanna and his wife three children to adopt: Shadrak, Meshak and Miriama. I never heard the stories of the adoptions.

Johanna did not tell me this, but he faced persecution when he first returned to the Kipsigis area in 1916 and tried to preach to the people there. I heard that one time his mother was dragged down the streets of Kericho by her hair because the people were so angry about Johanna's preaching. I also heard that at one point Johanna himself was nearly killed.

At that time, a government compound was about five miles from Tenwek. The compound was a fenced-in area and had been given the Kipsigis name of Bomet. Bomet means corral. The corral and the buildings are no longer there, but the name is still used for the Indian village and shops there now.

Johanna discovered a fellow Christian in the Bomet government compound when one of the English officers stationed there invited Johanna to stay in the fenced-in area for his own safety. He apparently lived there day and night for two years and preached to the Kipsigis as they came in to do business. During that two-year period, about one hundred people accepted Jesus as Savior. They went out and told their friends, and by the time Johanna could safely preach outside the compound, four churches already had been established.

Johanna's calling was first of all to be an evangelist, but as time went on, he developed another important ministry. He became a mentor to the missionary men, especially concerning the culture. If a problem arose and the missionaries were unsure how to solve it, Johanna was a good resource. He could explain the culture and predict how the people were going to react. He often came up with a good solution. Johanna did a lot of praying, too. I suppose he considered himself a prayer partner for every missionary at Tenwek station.

Because Johanna lived across the river from Tenwek, we easily could get his attention by just going outside and calling his name. He came over if there was a need. In the later years, his ministry for the doctor was not so much in person-to-person contact but through prayer. At night if Johanna saw the lights on at the hospital, it usually meant surgery, so he stayed awake and prayed until the lights went out.

Johanna passed away in 1977 at an undetermined age. If he had been 14 in 1902 when Karamoja Bell first came to Kenya to hunt and needed a gun bearer, Johanna would have been 89 when he died. That would have been very old for a man of his generation. My guess is that not many Kipsigis lived to 60 in those days. Health care of any kind was a relatively new thing. We do know he served the Lord well for 60 some years and certainly earned his rest. I'm thankful I got to know him in this life and look forward to seeing him again.

CHAPTER FOURTEEN
Odd Jobs

Although I could not understand the language, I started attending the Kipsigis church services right away after I arrived at Tenwek. I missed the presence of flowers in the church; so before long I was taking it upon myself to fix a bouquet and put it in front of the pulpit early Sunday morning.

One Sunday – it must have been during the dry season – I found few flowers to use. I picked a few purple irises and a few orange African daisies but not enough of either to make a good bouquet. So I put them together. I did not really like it – it seemed gaudy to me – but I took it down to the church anyway.

That morning for the first time several of the Africans told me how pretty the flowers were. I was surprised but thankful for this input, and I knew I would make more bouquets of purple irises and orange African daisies because the Kipsigis liked them.

• • •

I don't know how the Kipsigis parents teach their children to show no reaction to pain, but I know they start early. I remember one little 4-year-old boy who needed a shot in his buttock, and this required one of the large needles. His father had brought the boy in, and as I approached with the medication, the little boy reached for his daddy. The father made no move to pick him up but said quietly, "You're all right."

The boy stood still as I gave the shot. He made no attempt to jerk away from the pain and barely whimpered as I injected the medication. The father kept repeating softly, "You're all right. You're all right." I was impressed by the father's love and gentleness and the 4-year-old's maturity as he endured the pain.

• • •

One weekend, one of the African nurses, Esta, went home to see her parents, and while there she fell into a barbed wire fence and split her upper lip wide open. When I first saw Esta after this happened, she was not crying but was wailing as she rocked back and forth: "I have become bad, I have become bad, I have become bad."

And indeed, this beautiful young Kipsigis maiden had "become bad" because every time she spoke, that gash in her lip opened up into a wide inverted V, and her appearance was bad.

We had no surgical sutures or local anesthetics, but I knew I needed to do something to help Esta. In the end, I used white cotton thread and an ordinary sewing needle to close the wound.

Esta lay back on the examining table and remained totally relaxed and quiet while I took three or four stiches in her lip. Girls, as well as boys, are taught to endure pain quietly and without drama, and she passed the test one hundred percent.

We treated her wound the way we had cared for hair lip repairs in the States, and in the end she had a barely noticeable hairline scar. Esta had become "good" again!

A week or so later the doctor who was visiting Tenwek Hospital each month to meet the government requirement for a supervising doctor so the RNs could run a hospital, came on his regular visit, and I had him check Esta's lip. He was an Englishman, and he and his family were settlers in Kenya.

He said the sutures were ready to come out. I asked him if he wanted to take them out. His reply was, "No. You put them in; you can jolly well take them out!"

It was some time before I realized my mistake. In England, doctors do not take out sutures; nurses do that! I comfort myself by thinking that he probably knew enough about international medical practices to know that doctors in America take out sutures, and so he probably was not really insulted by my asking him do a nurse's job.

• • •

When Esta was to be married, she asked me to make her wedding bouquet. Years earlier, Trudie Shryock had planted a Sweetheart rose bush in our back yard. It was 5 or 6 feet across, and it bloomed pretty much the year round. Esta would have a bouquet of Sweetheart roses.

I made the bouquet and tied it together with some narrow pink ribbon I had. Streamers of pink ribbon fell 12 to 18 inches from the bouquet, and into the streamers I tied little Sweetheart rose buds. Esta loved it.

A number of times after that, a prospective bride came to me and said, "Amache taptok kou Esta." I think the best English translation for that would be "I want flowers a la Esta." So I made a number of those bouquets while I was in Kenya.

I like to think the Kipsigis are still making bouquets like that. And I can imagine a young Kipsigis bride-to-be asking her mother, "Why do we call the wedding bouquet 'taptok kou Esta'"? Maybe the mother will know and maybe she won't. But if she has ever lived in the area around Tenwek, she will probably know that Esta was the first to have a bouquet like the one I made.

• • •

One day while I was working in the dispensary at Cheptenye, the African nurse's aide came in, obviously disturbed about something. She called to me in what seemed to be a stage whisper, and she made the palm-down gesture that also asked me to come, "Misi Rosiman, Misi Rosiman, come." I stopped what I was doing and followed her.

Outside, the group of normally gregarious women were silently gathered in small groups looking at the sky. As I followed their gaze, I saw what appeared to be a white chalk mark silently proceeding across the blue dome of the sky from north to south. No cause for the continuing mark was noticeable. The mark seemed to be self-propelled.

Fortunately some of the missionaries returning from the States had told us about these marks and the new planes that made them. So I shaded my eyes and took another good look. Sure enough, I saw a tiny silver speck about a quarter of an inch ahead of the white chalk mark!

I told them that the mark was made by a plane, and I went back to finish what I had been doing in the dispensary. But I wish I had taken the time to help them see that plane.

However, they believed me and because I was unafraid, they were no longer afraid.

We heard later that near riots had taken place in Nairobi because of the big snake crawling across the sky!

• • •

One day David Kellogg, the missionary supervisor at Cheptenye station, called to me, "Millie, come here. I want to show you something." He had been walking toward the Land Rover, and when he got there, he lifted the hood and stood there waiting for me. I groaned inwardly; machinery was not my thing. I was unimpressed by motors, spark plugs, pipes and belts. In fact, I was more apt to be intimidated by them.

"If you are ever out somewhere and the Land Rover won't start, just get this screwdriver out of the glove compartment and scrape these posts on the battery," he said. Well, that looked simple enough, I thought as I noted the location of the posts so I would not scrape the wrong thing.

Sure enough, several weeks later, I had taken some women to a women's meeting 10 or 15 miles from Cheptenye, and when we got in the Land Rover to come back, it wouldn't start!

The women were well aware that the vehicle had not done its thing and that maybe it would be awhile before we got home. They voiced their alarm by saying, "Oh-aye, oh aye" over and over.

As I pulled the screwdriver out of the glove compartment, I prayed the Lord would help me remember and do the repair right.

When I got out and lifted the hood, the women became very confident and comforted each other by saying, "You say she doesn't know? She knows! You say she doesn't know? She knows!"

Fortunately the posts were in the place I remembered them to be, and they were corroded. So I started scraping. And I prayed, "Lord, please let this work. I don't have a back-up plan."

We could send a runner to get David to come and fix the Land Rover, but that would make everybody late getting home, and maybe the women would not be allowed to go to another afternoon meeting.

I probably scraped and prayed a little longer than necessary just to be sure. And when I got back in the driver's seat, I was still praying as I turned the key in the ignition. The Land Rover started! I heard many "Kongois" (thank yous) from the women as we started our journey home. And for about the next ten minutes they kept talking about how much I knew and how many things I could do. "You say she doesn't know? She knows!" I don't think they ever found out how inadequate I was in some areas.

I was thankful to the Lord for helping me get the women home in good time and thankful to David for giving me that one little lesson in vehicle maintenance.

Esta's wedding

CHAPTER FIFTEEN
A Doctor for Tenwek

For several years we had been hearing reports that a medical student in the U.S. hoped to come to Kenya as the doctor for Tenwek Hospital. This was exciting news, but past experience showed that doctors were often side-tracked. Understandably, they needed to pay off their student loans before taking an obscure job in a remote part of the world, a job that probably paid less than $100 a month. And once a doctor paid off the loans, the U.S. income looked so great compared to the income of a medical student or intern or the allowance of a missionary that the decision to stay in the States and help support missionaries instead of being one was all too easy to make.

So we were encouraged to not count on the doctor getting there any time soon. And with that we carried on, doing the best we could with what we had and sending the very ill into Kericho to be cared for at the government hospital.

Then one day in early 1959, we got word that Dr. and Mrs. Ernest Steury (Ernie & Sue) had been assigned to Tenwek and would arrive in a few months.

Missionaries customarily learned the language before starting to work, and our local leadership voted that the doctor should do his language study at the Bible School 50 miles away because, they reasoned, "If he's at Tenwek, the nurses will be frequently calling on him to help with the hard cases that come in."

I, for one was disappointed that he was going to be so far away, and I thought that we could all be careful and seldom bother him. But as the days went by and I noticed how many times I thought I would like to ask Ernie about one thing or another, I realized that those in charge had made the right decision.

After 6 months of language study, Ernie and Sue and their 3-year-old daughter moved into the other missionary house on the same terrace as Freedom Hall.

When Ernie came on board, the hospital staff consisted of two nurses, Betty and me; one American lab technician, Amy; one Kipsigis lab technician, Ezekiel, who had trained at the big King George VI hospital in Nairobi; and a dozen or so Kipsigis nurses' aides.

Each morning while we made rounds, one of the Kipsigis girls listed the patients to be seen along with their main complaint. Ernie chose the most difficult ones and saw them, and Betty and I took the others.

If any of the patients needed special treatment or care that required more than one person – such as surgery – Ernie found us, let us know what needed to be done and we prepared for and did that procedure before seeing the rest of the new patients.

One such morning about 10:00, Ernie came looking for us with a problem. He had a young mother and a baby about 18 months old with him. He had just diagnosed the child's problem: peritonsillar abscesses, which were slowly closing off the child's airway. She was already having difficulty breathing, and Ernie had outlined his treatment plan to the mother. He would make a small slit in the child's throat and insert a tube so the child could breathe easily while we treated the infection and made her well.

The mother was frightened and did not want to give permission for the procedure. Instead, she offered to run home (probably about 5 miles one way) and bring her husband back to make the decision. Ernie told her we didn't have time for that; by the time she returned, the child would be dead.

My heart went out to the mother as I watched her struggle. Who knows what would happen to her if her husband concluded she had made the wrong decision and the child died as a result? Nor did she want to stand by and watch as the child died.

Gently, Ernie kept telling her we needed to do the procedure so the baby wouldn't have such a struggle to breathe. Eventually, she reluctantly gave permission in front of Kipsigis witnesses, and Ernie was able to do the relatively simple surgery and ease the child's distress.

Antibiotics took care of the abscesses, and in about a week they were shrunk to the point that we could remove the tracheotomy tube and close the wound. When Ernie told the mother we were going to take out the tube, she said fearfully, "No, no, no! She won't be able to breathe without that!"

Once again, we had to convince her to let us do what we knew to be the right thing for the child. We told her she could stay for a few days until we were sure everything was all right. She finally agreed, and in a few days she went home with a healthy little girl.

Whenever the child had a physical problem, the mother brought her in to the hospital. She always pulled back clothing so we could see the scar and know that this was the one who had the tube in her throat.

CHAPTER SIXTEEN
Arap Segem

A few months after Ernie joined the hospital staff, he came looking for Betty and me one morning. He said we were going to have to do something we had never done before, and we needed to get started right away.

Ernie had just admitted an elderly looking man named Arap Segem who, according to his history, had been very sick at home for several weeks. He seemed to be recovering but suddenly started bleeding rectally. He was going to need surgery ASAP, and he was going to need blood transfusions or he probably would not make it.

We had never done a blood transfusion.

In his equipment from the States, Ernie had bottles and tubing for four transfusions. We would have to pray that four transfusions would be enough for Arap Segem. Our first order of business was to find four donors. Ernie ruled out letting any of the medical staff (American or African) donate because we were all exposed to many diseases every day.

Next we looked at the rest of the missionaries. That was easy. Each one knew his or her blood type already and didn't have to have it "typed" to find out if it was useable. One missionary, Gene Lewton, was a universal donor. He would give the first unit of blood.

Ernie checked the gardener who cared for the hospital grounds. He had the right type but wasn't sure he wanted anything to do with giving his blood to someone else. So I told him he could have the rest of the day off if he gave us some blood, and he was happy and agreed to do it.

About that time I got a call from the Indian Village, Bomet, 5 miles down the road. Someone there wanted to see the doctor, but it was not an emergency. So I told the caller what was going on and asked the patient to come the next morning.

Ernie was still checking anyone who was healthy and seemed interested in donating but was having little luck finding people with the right type of blood when a big flatbed truck with sideboards pulled in. Standing on the bed of that truck were 20 or 30 Indians from Bomet, mostly men, but a few women. They started unloading immediately.

Didn't I explain they were to come tomorrow? I thought as I went out to meet them. As the first group came closer, I said, a bit reproachfully, "Didn't we agree that you would come tomorrow morning?"

"No, no," one of the men said. "We have come to help."

My face must have registered a lack of comprehension because he quickly added, "With the blood – we can help?"

He was watching me closely to see if I would accept their offer. And it seemed to be important to them that they be allowed to help.

"Oh," I said, "OK. Let me go tell the doctor."

Ernie and the lab technician worked quickly to draw blood and type it, and before long they had two more donors!

As I think back on this incident, I marvel that all three cultures (European, Asian and African) came together to help one man whom none of us had ever met before.

Arap Segem had come from near the border of Kipsigis territory – probably 20 or 30 miles from Tenwek – and so I assume he had come by ox-sled or some similar form of transportation. He was accompanied by his three wives. No children were with them, and that probably meant all three of the wives were beyond child-bearing age. Determining their ages was hard for us, but I'm guessing that all four of them were in their late 50s or early 60s.

The three wives were very quiet and tended to stay close together. They seemed to have a good bond between the three of them and also an interdependence that supported and encouraged each other. None of the four seemed frightened of the surgery.

Ernie's pre-surgery diagnosis was typhoid fever with resulting intestinal lesions (called Peyer's Patches) that were bleeding and would not stop bleeding on their own. Instead, they were likely to cause perforations in the intestinal wall.

I have little recollection of our preparation for that surgery. I suppose Ernie drew the blood ahead of time and then refrigerated it until needed.

Was the big sterilizer ready for use yet? I don't remember. If not, we sterilized the instruments, etc. in Sue's pressure cooker.

Our "surgery" was so primitive I'm almost ashamed to tell you about it. The room was small (10 feet x 10 feet) and had no running water. We did have electricity. Our surgery was not inside a nice clean building, but opened directly to the outside where there were often people, even sick people. Because it was our surgery, we kept the door and windows shut at all times except when we needed to go through the door.

The windows were high and on two sides of the room only. Everybody at the hospital knew when we were doing a surgery, and in a short time other patients or family members placed boxes or blocks of wood below the surgery windows, and people stood on them so they could watch what we were doing inside. In a way this was a good thing because Ernie had nothing to hide, and the more the Africans understood what Ernie was doing, the faster they would trust him.

We had no plumbing at the hospital and so "scrubbing" before surgery was a problem. We "scrubbed" in boiled water in a granite basin that also had been boiled, using a stiff-bristled brush that had been sterilized and a new bar of soap. After scrubbing for the prescribed number of minutes, one of the nurses' aides poured cooled boiled water over our hands and arms, and we dried them with a sterilized towel. We scrubbed in a room next to the surgery, but we had to go outside and walk a few steps to go into the surgery room. nurses' aides were there to open and close the doors because we could not touch anything.

One time after I had scrubbed, as I stepped out the door, a drop of water fell from the roof onto my hand, and I had to go back and scrub again!

Betty and I were the only nurses available, so one of us gave the anesthetic under Ernie's watchful eye, and the other was the instrument nurse. Almost from the beginning Ernie included one of the African nurses' aides in that first surgical team. That nurse was Esta, the girl whose lip I had repaired. She could do many things to help, and she learned fast.

Ernie's habit was to pray with each patient before surgery. He briefly explained the plan of salvation, asked if he or she would like to accept Jesus as Savior right then, and followed with a short prayer for health and recovery for the patient and for wisdom and guidance for us. Often he ended his prayer with the phrase "and may Christ have the pre-eminence."

We started the first unit of blood before we started the surgery. Arap Segem's blood pressure remained good all during the surgery, and by mid-afternoon we returned him to the big ward and to the care of his wives. He had an IV going, and his wives had been instructed not to give him anything to eat or drink until the doctor said it was all right to feed him.

He made a good recovery and in a few days was off the IV and up and around.

Every day except Sunday we had a service in the chapel. Usually one of the local African pastors spoke, and we expected all ambulatory patients to attend. Arap Segem and his wives attended, and one day he stayed after the service, prayed with the pastor and accepted Jesus as his Savior. He told his wives they were now going to be a Christian family.

When Arap Segem was strong enough, he was discharged, and the grateful family returned home.

About three weeks later, Arap Segem returned to Tenwek; he was bleeding again. Unfortunately, Ernie and I were in Nairobi attending the annual medical meetings for Kenya. Betty offered to take him and his wives to the government hospital in Kericho, but he refused, saying, "Tenwek has become my home; I will die at Tenwek."

The Kipsigis believe evil spirits are all around, and they come at the time of a death and take that person away. But sometimes the evil spirits make a mistake and take the wrong person; so there is much fear at the time of a death. Kipsigis women usually left the scene of a death, running as fast as they could and screaming at the top of their voices.

The fear of evil spirits extends into other parts of their lives. The Kipsigis built round houses because they believe that the spirits like to hide in corners. Expectant mothers make no preparation for the new baby because they don't want to let the evil spirits know a baby is coming. If the spirits know a baby is expected, they will be prepared to snatch it away. And, if a mother has lost several babies, she will name the next one Machi (Not a Person) in an attempt to make the evil spirits think the new baby is unimportant and not worth taking.

The Kipsigis also believe evil spirits get in the body and cause disease. To remedy that, they make little cuts in the skin over the affected area to let the spirits out. These little cuts were often the reason that tetanus developed. When examining adult patients, we jokingly referred to the medical history that we found "written" on the chest and abdomen.

When one of the African nurses came to tell Betty that Arap Segem had died, she went up to the hospital to see if she could be of any help. As she walked into the room, she saw the three wives standing around the bed, praying.

Betty was impressed; so was I when she told me about it. I've always been intrigued by the changes in people's lives after they have accepted Jesus as Savior, and this was an unusual example. These women were believers because their husband made the decision and told them they were part of it. They accepted that, and the Lord gave them faith and understanding, and in only three weeks' time their lives were changed. They could face widowhood unafraid and look to the Lord for guidance in the days ahead.

I do believe that if I had not already accepted Jesus as my Savior before this happened, I would have done it then because this was such a striking change to occur in four lives all at once.

Arap Segem probably traveled to Tenwek on an ox-sled similar to this one.

CHAPTER SEVENTEEN
Second Furlough

During my last two years in Kenya (1959-1960), I had dysentery most of the time. Lab tests proved that I had an amoebic infection. At that time, my diet consisted of meat and potatoes or rice, bread (especially bread and gravy), dairy products and cereals. Fruits and most vegetables were contributing to the problem; so I eliminated them from my diet. I remember one morning when I was feeling better, and I put some jam on my toast. Before the end of the day, I knew I had made the wrong decision.

Surprisingly I was never sick enough to go to bed, and I maintained a fairly good energy level. I lost between ten and fifteen pounds, however.

I had talked to Dr. Probst about the dysentery several times. He was the Africa Inland Mission doctor who came to Tenwek once a month to help us with the difficult cases and meet the government requirements that allowed RNs to run a "hospital." One time when I was complaining about my limited diet, he said, not at all encouragingly, "Well, some people just can't ever eat normally again."

Somewhere during this time, an unsettling experience occurred and left a dim memory in my mind. The facts and personalities involved are unclear, but I remember my feelings very well. Several of the missionaries, including me, were in one of our vehicles returning to Tenwek. We started talking about something that had happened at the hospital. Two African families were part of our discussion. One of the women had recently been a patient in our maternity ward – with twins, I think. At least something a bit unusual. I remember nothing about the other African family.

We arrived at Tenwek and started unloading right after I had made a number of statements about what had happened. As I got out of the vehicle and started toward our house, I realized that I had the facts about those two families all mixed up, and I had been talking about the wrong woman having been in the maternity ward. I was embarrassed that the others in the car probably had been aware of my confusion and break with reality.

No one said anything about it at the time. I have no recollection of ever talking about the incident again, and I do feel that the confusion was a result of the strain of all the responsibility we felt in the medical work.

And then my routine TB skin test showed positive!

Sometime later the decision was made that I should come home early. I do not remember how that decision was made – I just remember packing. As I packed my things to leave, I had the feeling I might not be returning. I packed a couple of barrels to be shipped to me later if I did stay in America.

With the work at the hospital and packing, I was totally exhausted by the time I boarded the plane. As I recall, we left Nairobi in the early evening. I think I fell asleep within the first half hour after takeoff and woke up as we were flying into Rome the next morning. The passenger sitting beside me said she had worried about me all night because I wasn't waking up.

From Rome we flew to London and then changed planes for New York. I stopped for a few days in Indianapolis to see a man with whom I had been corresponding for about a year. We originally had met ten years earlier in 1950. This was a renewed relationship when he started writing again and looked promising. But when we met face to face again, nothing clicked. No doubt my illnesses were a large factor; I also think spending several years in another culture changes people in subtle ways. After a few days we broke up, and I went on to Oregon.

I got home in late August. On Labor Day, my parents and I went to the State Fair, and the temperature reached 98 degrees. After living in the Kenya Highlands, I wasn't used to that!

Once again I was excited to be home, and I enjoyed seeing many of my friends. But after a few weeks, doing almost nothing got old. I felt I was too young to be put on the shelf. So I left the farm west of Beaverton where my folks were still living, rented an apartment in Portland and went back to work at Emanuel Hospital, the hospital where I had trained to be a nurse.

Some people, when they heard I was working, were surprised and said, "We thought you came home to rest." But what they did not understand was the differences between the work at Tenwek and the work at Emanuel. At Emanuel I worked an eight-hour shift and followed doctors' orders. Doctors made all the important decisions. When I went home, I knew I was not going to be called back for any emergency.

Once, when I was the only nurse at Tenwek, I kept track of how many times I was called out at night. The average was ten times a week. Some nights, I was up several times and got just a few hours' sleep. Occasionally, I got a full night's sleep.

Back in America, I was getting adequate rest between shifts, and, although I was having to learn or relearn some things, I enjoyed being on duty, and the work was good for me. It gave me something to think about besides a failed romance.

During the first few months I was home, I worked on gaining weight – the only time in my life I ever had to do that! After three months, people started commenting on how much better I looked than I did when I first came home.

I had one course of treatment for the dysentery, and that solved that problem. The follow-up for the tuberculosis showed I had a small spot that my immune system had walled off. The expectation was the organisms would die off, and I would have no problems from the short-lived infection. That seems to be what happened. Annual chest X-rays showed no further lesions.

I don't remember when I started taking speaking engagements. I had some while I was still working at Emanuel. Because the hospital had a shortage of hospital nurses, the nursing director let me work around my speaking schedule.

What to include when I had an opportunity to speak was easier this second furlough. Tenwek now had a doctor. That was a big answer to prayer and gave the mission a greatly expanded outreach to share the gospel with the Kipsigis people. The story of Arap Segem, his three wives, his blood transfusions and his conversion was a good way of demonstrating the value of having a doctor at Tenwek.

Usually the people just wanted a missionary message, but I remember one time when I was asked to talk about the language. At first I thought I would have little to say, but I found language made a good subject. I shared many interesting things including that the Kipsigis language had been influenced by the tribe's time in Egypt (Kipsigis is a Nilo-Hamitic language). I also told about little John Clark who was slow in developing his talking skills. But then suddenly, when he was 3, he demonstrated he could speak 3 different languages: English, Kipsigis and Swahili.

In the spring of 1961, I got a phone call from a man named Leonard Gackle. He had heard me speak at the Wichita Avenue Evangelical Church where he attended regularly and also heard me speak at another church later that week. He was calling to ask me out on a date! Here I was, 36 years old and had not had a date in America for a long, long time!

I told him I would have to check my speaking schedule and call him back. The mission representative in the Northwest who was in charge of scheduling meetings in Oregon for the missionaries on furlough attended the same church that Leonard did. So when I called to see if he had scheduled any meetings for me, I asked about Leonard. I was told by the lady of the house, "Oh, he's nice. You'll like him!" So I accepted the invitation and went out with him.

Our first date was (would you believe?) to a missionary meeting! I don't remember who was speaking, but I do remember the pleasure of listening to someone else's experience on a mission field. The evening was enjoyable.

Our second date was an Easter sunrise service. After the service, we shared a leisurely breakfast at a small restaurant before going to Sunday school and church. While we were eating, Leonard looked at me intently and asked with a chuckle, "You called Mrs. Moore and asked her about me, didn't you?" I admitted I had asked about him when I called to check on my schedule.

Then he asked with a big smile, "If you hadn't had anybody to ask, would you have gone out with me?" Well, yes, I probably would have because he was obviously interested in missions.

Leonard was Canadian and had been in the States on a student visa, but that fall, because he was no longer in school, he went back to Canada and applied for a permanent visa to the U.S. When Leonard first got back to Canada, he was offered a job for $2.00 an hour and turned it down because he thought he could do better. But it was winter, and no other suitable jobs became available, so he was unemployed for six or seven months. He divided his time between his folks' farm in Saskatchewan and his sister Alice's place in Medicine Hat, Alberta.

We wrote to each other weekly and occasionally talked on the phone. Later that winter, I flew to Medicine Hat for a short visit. Seeing Leonard in person again was much better than talking on the phone! It was nice to see the farm where he grew up and to meet his family. His parents spoke German most of the time with their family, but when I came into the room, they switched to English so I could understand, too. They made me feel very welcome.

One of the fun things we did while I was there was to go to a curling game in an ice rink in Medicine Hat. In this game, each team propels a man-made stone (with a handle on top of it) sliding down the ice to a target laid out under the ice. Other team members try to direct, slow down or speed up the stone's progress by quickly sweeping the ice in front of the stone without actually touching the stone as it moves along. I had never even heard of curling before that trip.

A few months later, Leonard was granted a permanent visa to the United States and returned to Oregon. He was hired at Riverview Abbey where several other Canadians whom he knew were working.

Sometime, in early 1962 I think it was, I got a letter from World Gospel Mission telling me the board had taken a vote and decided I should not go back to Kenya. Although I had felt when I left Kenya that I might not be returning, I was feeling much better physically by the time the letter arrived, and so the news came as quite a surprise.

My feelings were mixed. I was disappointed I would not be returning to Kenya and in many ways felt like a failure, but at the same time this opened up the opportunity to pursue my relationship with Leonard.

I told no one except my parents and Leonard that the decision to stay in America was more than just my own decision. My response to the situation was to pack it up and store it away in the back of my mind. As the years passed, I did not even think much about this turn of events. I'm not sure this was the best way to handle the situation, but that is what I did.

I'm thankful I maintained a good relationship with the mission and the missionaries with whom I had worked.

During the earlier months of my furlough before that letter came, I had made no plans for what I would do if I stayed in America. Soon I was writing lists – things I could do, where I could live, what opportunities I could take advantage of, etc. The only things I remember from those lists are 1) to continue working at Emanuel Hospital, 2) to live and work in Astoria near my sister and her family, or 3) to go back to school and get my degree in nursing.

Because Leonard and I were still dating, I stayed in Portland and continued working at Emanuel. As our relationship became more serious, we discussed the possibility of marriage and a family. That Christmas (1962) he gave me a beautiful engagement ring, and we were married the next year on October 5th.

Leonard Gackle and Millie were married on October 5, 1963.

CHAPTER EIGHTEEN
Extended Ministry

After Leonard and I were married, we lived in my apartment near Emanuel for about a year and then moved to a rented house in Milwaukie.

Our daughter, Patricia Rose, was born Friday, November 13, 1964 – and ten days later I turned 40!

David Winston was born April 6, 1967. When he was two months old, we moved to the Willamette area of West Linn. We had bought a small house with almost two acres. It had a nice sothern slope. The bottom part of the property, the remnants of an old family orchard, was mostly covered with a dense growth of Himalaya blackberries. Those we fought for the next 31 years.

Because we had moved farther away from the Wichita Avenue Evangelical Church, we transferred to the Oregon City Evangelical Church when our daughter was starting junior high.

From the time we started attending there, Leonard and I went to the Wednesday evening prayer meeting, and Patricia attended the youth group. The church had no program for the younger children. They played with little supervision in the nursery next to the room the adults used.

A few weeks later, the pastor asked the mothers to take turns teaching and supervising the six or eight children parents brought every week. So, of course, I took my turn. After a couple months, most of the mothers had dropped out, and only two of us were left. After a few more weeks, I was teaching lessons every week.

One Sunday evening during the service, the pastor surprised me by saying the younger children were having a Bible study every Wednesday night. I didn't see what I was doing as a "Bible study" because the lessons had no continuity, but I did want to provide a real Bible study for the children. Immediately my mind went to the Old Testament, and I asked the Lord to show me what He wanted me to teach. I thought of the divided kingdom and went backward from there through the reigns of Solomon, David and Saul, the time of the judges, the conquest of the Promised Land, the exodus – that's what we would study! We would start with the birth of Moses and go through his early life, his exile, his call and continue on with the ten plagues and the crossing of the Red Sea.

I was excited about this plan and started on it right away. The children loved it. We even included a simple study of the Tabernacle in the lessons. We ended the Old Testament lessons with the death of Moses and then took on the book of Luke.

I taught that class of 12 to 15 students (from kindergarteners to sixth graders) for about 2 years. Then one Sunday morning, the pastor's wife asked me if instead of teaching the children, I would consider teaching the women's Bible study starting that fall.

"Oh, I'd love to," I said.

But as I thought about it later that day, I felt totally inadequate and unprepared to teach. So that evening I told her I had reconsidered and thought I should not do it. But she convinced me to try – and promised to pray for me. So I finally agreed. The women met in small groups to discuss the lesson, and then I lectured 30-40 minutes covering the same material. Although the preparation was time-consuming, I loved teaching and probably learned more than anyone else in the class. I taught that women's Bible study for nine years and then quit to give someone else the opportunity.

A couple of years after Patricia and David were both out of high school, we applied to go as a family on a work team to Kenya. I wanted Leonard and our children to see Kenya and experience life on a mission station. I think the team was to go in the late fall. The people in charge wanted to know about our abilities and training. I filled out the application for all of us. Leonard was a good repair man and mechanic: He could improvise and fix almost anything. Patricia was studying to be an occupational therapist. She was young and strong, a committed Christian and willing worker; she could and would do almost anything. David had several years' experience as a roofer, and when I put that down on paper, I could not resist the temptation to add that he didn't do grass roofs.

As I considered my own abilities, I realized I was probably the least qualified. I was pushing 60 and already experiencing some physical problems that were slowing me down and calling for frequent breaks. I would be the one contributing the least from our family. But maybe I could help with the team's cooking and laundry.

Several weeks before we were to leave, we got a phone call from the office saying the trip had been cancelled because too few people had signed up to go. The mission would let us know when another trip was planned.

No letter came, but sometime in January I think it was, someone from the mission office phoned. The person wanted to know if we were planning to go with the work team to Kenya. I asked about the dates. Departure was just a few weeks away – not really time to arrange for time off and other preparations. So I told them we were unable to go at that time.

I wondered why the mission had waited so long to contact us. Then in March we got a letter telling about the work team I had turned down in January. The letter was postmarked sometime in November and did not reach us until March! We felt the Lord had been in control of that lost letter, and this just meant we were not supposed to be on that team. Somehow we all got busy and never tried to plan such a family trip again.

Our marriage, like all marriages, had its ups and downs. I did not realize it when we got married, but Leonard and I came from two very different cultures. Although he was Canadian, he had been raised in an Old-World German community and culture. He spoke German until he went to school and then learned English as a second language.

The early years of our marriage were strained. Those years remind me of the often-used analogy for marriage – a rock tumbler that causes semi-precious stones to constantly bump each other until each is polished and beautiful. During those years, I sometimes felt my love for Leonard was being destroyed, but in the end, it came back stronger than before.

As the years went by, I found many things to appreciate about Leonard.

I loved him for being a good and faithful provider. I loved him for seeing that church attendance for our family was consistent. I loved him for being frugal and not spending money we did not have – and for teaching that concept to our children. I loved him for making sure our children got the training necessary for good-paying jobs. I loved him for supporting missionaries. I loved him for being a good gardener and for sharing his produce generously. And I loved him for the little things I liked that had not been part of his early life – such as cards and flowers.

We celebrated our marriage several times. The first was our 25th anniversary. I made it a point to celebrate our 40th because, at our ages, I thought we probably would not make it to 50. We did make it to 50; so we celebrated again. Our last celebration was our 51st, and that was in the hospital with a cake and our immediate family six days before Leonard passed away.

CHAPTER NINETEEN
Joseph Rono

A few years later in the early 1980s, one of the Kipsigis pastors came to the United States to attend Western Evangelical Seminary. His name was Joseph Arap Rono. He would be living in Milwaukie and attending the same church we did. I remember his first Sunday evening here. He was introduced to the congregation, and he asked us to pray with him that when he finished his schooling, he would still be willing to go back to Kenya to serve his people.

When Joseph arrived, I started introducing him as Joseph Arap Rono. He told me the Kipsigis had stopped using the Arap in their names; so now his name was simply Joseph Rono. Rono would be passed on in his family as the surname. This was a good change and would make tracing family histories much easier.

Joseph was from another part of the Kipsigis area, and I had never met him, but I wanted to get to know him. I planned to invite him for Thanksgiving dinner. So on the first Sunday of November, I told him we wanted him to come for Thanksgiving and spend the day with our family. His first response was "I'll have to check and see if we have classes that day." Slowly, I realized why he would need to check. He had been in America only about five weeks, and he didn't know what an important holiday Thanksgiving was in our culture. Then he got a puzzled look on his face and asked, "Last night I had children knocking on my door…?"

Halloween! And nobody had prepared him for that! I felt terrible. I knew both cultures, and I should have thought to warn him. I determined right then to explain all of our holidays to him before they happened. But, unfortunately, it was sort of like locking the barn door after the horse was stolen! No other holidays are like Halloween.

Joseph said he didn't know what the children wanted, and he didn't know what to do, so he turned off the light and went to bed.

Thanksgiving turned out to be an enjoyable day. My sister and her family and my mother were also at our home. While the ladies were getting dinner ready, the men and children watched television. Pictures of skiing on snowy slopes came on, and Joseph had lots of questions. Our son, David, who was about 15, brought out his skis and explained skis and skiing to Joseph. He seemed to understand and enjoyed talking with David about it. Joseph inspected the skis very thoroughly.

In the weeks that followed, we fell into the habit of spending Sunday afternoon with Joseph. I was working part time at Willamette Falls Hospital in Oregon City, and that meant working every other Sunday. If I was not working, we had dinner at our house, but if I was working, Leonard took our children and Joseph to an all-you-can eat restaurant and then back to our house. We got well acquainted with Joseph and learned much about his history during those days.

Joseph had been orphaned when he was ten years old. His father had died some time earlier, and the father's brother, who should have taken responsibility for Joseph and his mother, refused to do so. Joseph's mother was so overwhelmed with the situation that she became despondent and committed suicide.

Joseph went to live with an aunt who was a Christian, and before long, Joseph accepted Jesus as his Savior, too.

When he was 14, Joseph started school. He loved learning and went through primary school, secondary school, and Bible school. Then he went on to Oregon to attend seminary.

When he was a young adult, he fell in love with a lovely young Kipsigis girl named Esther. When he talked with her father about marrying her, Joseph got a very cold reception. The father felt Joseph was a poor candidate for marriage. After all, he had no land and no cows for the bride price!

Joseph talked the situation over with Esther, and she promised to wait for him. Then he bought some calves and got permission to keep them at a friend's place and let them graze with the friend's herd while Joseph went on with his schooling. A couple of years later, Joseph had the cows for the bride price, and he and Esther were married.

The Kipsigis did not keep track of their ages once they became adults; so Joseph did not know how old he was. Once, when he was filling out some forms in a government office in Kenya, the clerk asked him how old he was. When Joseph didn't know, the clerk said, "We'll give you an age. You are 40." Joseph accepted that and added to it year by year.

However, Joseph gave great credibility to a story about his mother. It is told that when she was carrying Joseph and obviously pregnant, two men who claimed to be Mau Mau activists stopped her on the path one day. They discussed killing her, taking out the fetus and using it in their rituals. Surprisingly, something happened – and we don't know what – to make them change their minds. So they let her go. If that did happen, Joseph would have been born in the early 1950s and would have been about 30 when he first came to Oregon.

After four years, Joseph was ready to graduate from the seminary. Some of the people in our church raised money to bring Esther to America for the graduation. Joseph was thrilled. He obviously loved her very much and often referred to her as "my lady."

One day Leonard asked Joseph what he was going to do when he first saw Esther – maybe a big hug?

"No, we don't hug," he said. Joseph smiled at the thought. "If we've been apart for a long time, we might shake hands."

The night of Esther's arrival finally came, and we took Joseph to the airport to get her. Her plane from New York was delayed; so she missed a connecting flight. We waited a few more hours in great anticipation. None of us slept.

Finally her plane arrived. Joseph was waiting near the top of the ramp where the disembarking passengers would enter the building. Suddenly she came around the corner and saw Joseph. She squealed and started running. Joseph ran too, and when they were close enough, they went into the most American, unKipsigis hug you can imagine! Leonard and I had to wait a few more minutes before we got to meet Joseph's lady.

They sat in the back seat and talked quietly in Kipsigis all the way home. Joseph told me the next day that they had talked all night.

"You mean you didn't get any sleep?" I asked.

"Of course," Joseph answered as though that was not unusual at all.

After graduation we had a reception for Joseph at our house. About 50 people came to our little house and there were some rain showers that afternoon! Fortunately, a wide overhang across the front of the house which offered protection, many of the men congregated there.

Esther told me that in one of the airports, she had to walk quite a distance to get her next flight. Because it was easier for her and she could go faster, she put her carry-on bag on her head. She said people lo-o-o-o-oked at her as she hurried along. So when they left, I had her put her bag on her head and pose for a picture.

Joseph's assignment in Kenya was to be the administrative secretary and later bishop of all the Kipsigis churches founded by World Gospel Mission. That meant he supervised about 1,700 churches including quite a few outside the tribal area. It was an enormous task, and Joseph did it well as long as he was able. I'm sure Esther's secretarial skills were a big help to him.

Joseph passed away a number of years ago and left some pretty big sandals to fill. Fortunately, many Kenyans have experienced redemption through Jesus, and the Lord has called some of them to be the spiritual leaders of the country, and the church continues to grow.

Esther and Joseph Rono with Leonard Gackle. Joseph and Esther. were leaving Portland to return to Kenya.

Esther demonstrates the best way to hurry to catch her next flight.

CHAPTER TWENTY
Patrick Marunga and Family

A few years later, another pastor, Patrick Marunga, and his wife, Bea, came to the United States for further training. This couple came from Nairobi, and neither one was Kipsigis nor were the two of them from the same tribe. They grew up each speaking their own tribal language plus English and Swahili. I'm assuming they spoke more English than anything else in their home. They had a 3 year-old son, Jonathan or J.J., with them and he spoke English as well.

Patrick had gone to our Bible School in Kericho, Kenya Highlands Bible College. Because Patrick was always friendly and social, he wanted to talk to people. So while at the Bible College he learned to speak Kipsigis as a fourth language. After he met me, he always greeted me in Kipsigis, and I loved it.

Patrick was pastor of a big inter-racial church in Nairobi called Good Shepherd Church. He came to America to go to Western Evangelical Seminary, and our church also hired him as an intern during his time here. He worked mostly with the young adults and made some lasting friendships. Because he was spending so much time with the young adults, Leonard and I did fewer things with Patrick and Bea than we had with Joseph, but we did get to know him and his wife fairly well.

I was on the committee to furnish the house for them before they arrived. A few days after they moved in, Bea told one of the committee members that she would like to have a blender. I thought of the Kipsigis women – they wouldn't know what a blender was and would not have electricity to operate one! But Bea had grown up in Nairobi where the electricity was dependable, and she had learned to cook with a blender. No little pronged stick from the forest to keep this woman's porridge from being lumpy! We got her a blender.

Bea also took classes at the seminary and went back to Kenya a qualified Christian counselor.

We learned from Patrick that his father had been a successful businessman in Nairobi. Some other African businessmen there became jealous and accused Patrick's father of wrong-doing. As a result, Patrick's father was convicted and spent 1 ½ years in prison.

"But," Patrick said and smiled as he continued the story, "that's why we are Christians. My father became a Christian while he was in jail."

One day, while Patrick and Bea were still in Oregon, word came that Patrick's father had been in an automobile accident and was badly hurt. After weeks of treatment, he survived but was left crippled.

Several months later, I asked Patrick about his father and his quick response was, "Oh, he's fine!" I must have looked surprised because he added, "Oh, physically he's not doing very well, but spiritually, he's fine."

I had to admire Patrick for thinking of his father's spiritual condition before thinking of his physical condition, and I wanted to make that a habit in my own conversations. But somehow I've never managed to make that change. When the question of "How are you?" comes up, I always think of my physical or emotional well-being before I think of the spiritual well-being, which is much more important.

Patrick and Bea had their second son, Brian, while they were here. Now Brian is grown and back in Oregon going to school. He plans to become an architect and return to Kenya to work there.

When Patrick and Bea returned to Kenya, Patrick assumed the pastorate of the Good Shepherd Church for fifteen more years before resigning to work full-time at a theological seminary. He founded a ministry to Kenyan children infected or affected by HIV and AIDS. Patrick, with help from Americans, built a small village and staffed it with willing African grandmothers who provided loving homes and care for the AIDS orphans.

Patrick and Bea have also been instrumental in helping to resolve some inter-tribal tensions that have developed in recent years.

What a privilege to have known these two choice servants of the Lord!

CHAPTER TWENTY-ONE
Bob Nyanja

In 1998 we moved off of our almost two acres in West Linn to a city lot in Milwaukie, Oregon. I think it was early in the very next January that our pastor called to say a young African man was coming to the Portland area to take a six-week class in editing film by computer, and he was looking for a place to stay. He was already in the States, had planned one or two short visits between New York and Portland and would fly into Portland in three days. Would we be interested in having him stay with us?

Because we were both retired, because we had very little outside work to do in January and because this young man was from Kenya, we decided very quickly we wanted him to stay with us!

We fixed up the guest room for him – even emptied and moved in my little desk so he would have a place to do his homework if he had any.

Bob had said for us not to meet him at the airport. He would find his own way to our house because did not want to be a bother. However, we felt it would be best if we picked him up; so, we made a big sign almost four feet long that said BOB NYANJA and waited inside near the area where his plane would land. It was a slow time at the airport. Few people were around; so we were unafraid of missing him.

One well-dressed man who looked as if he could have recently flown in from Africa came by and stopped when we said "Bob?" He looked at us questioningly, shook his head and went on his way smiling.

The next man we saw who could be Bob was young and dressed like an American college student. His face lit up when he heard his name and then saw it on the sign. As we walked toward the baggage claim area, Bob looked back and forth at us and said, "The pastor said I would be staying with a retired couple?" We assured him we were retired, and he looked surprised. We realized the Africans must have as much trouble guessing our ages as we have guessing theirs!

The next day was Sunday. In the afternoon, we showed Bob where to wait about a block from our house to catch his bus; then we drove him downtown to see the place where he would transfer to another bus to take him to his class. Actually, we were being over-protective. Bob had spent two or three years at Bob Jones University and was unintimidated by American cities and their public transportation.

But the next day we worried off and on all day, wondering if he got on the right bus, if he got to his class on time, and if he was going to make it back to our house all right. We were as concerned as parents who had just sent their child off on a first date! He was later getting back than we had expected, and it had been dark for quite a while before he returned. But he made it back safely and reported he had had a good day. Leonard and I had already eaten, so I fixed a plate for Bob while we continued to question him about how he had fared. After Bob had almost finished his dinner, he abruptly stopped eating and looked from one to the other of us intently as he said, "Oh, I am so blessed! Most of the people in that class are staying in hotels. They were going to have to go out to eat and then back to their hotels. I am so blessed to have a home to come to."

I asked Bob if he had been warm enough. He hadn't. Leonard was always cold and had a good supply of jackets, and, although Bob was taller than Leonard, their shoulder width was about the same.

They found a warm, almost new gray jacket that Bob used while he was in Oregon. He had been warned about Oregon's rain and had brought an umbrella.

I knew very little about computers, and it blew my mind to think that here was a young man from a Third-World country who knew enough about computers to take a class in using them to edit film!

As we got to know Bob, we learned he was a photographer and had his own business in Nairobi. He even carried a pack of nicely done business cards.

We also learned Bob and Patrick were friends. They had grown up together, playing basketball on the side streets of Nairobi. An older European couple in the area invited groups of those "street boys" into their home for snacks, games and discussions about Jesus. Through their influence, Bob became a Christian.

One day when Bob didn't have classes, he started talking about politics – Kenyan politics and American politics. I was surprised how much he knew about our government. After we had talked for some time, I said, "You ought to run for president of Kenya."

His quick and emphatic response was, "Well, I just might!" So someday you may hear his name in the news.

Sometime after Bob went back to Kenya, we heard he had been one of the photographers for the "Survivor" series when it was filmed in Kenya. I tried to think back on the pictures I had seen of that and wondered which ones Bob had taken. I remembered the "survivors" had built a boma (corral) out of brush around their little encampment. The boma looked very unsubstantial, and one night a photographer filmed a lioness walking around the boma's perimeter. Probably she didn't jump over because she didn't know how wide the pile of brush was or what was on the other side.

Later a report came out in a magazine about a time when the photographers were laughing so hard they could hardly operate their cameras. The "survivors" were supposed to move some goats from one place to another, and they were having little success. The goats were noticeably uncooperative, and the "survivors" were noticeably inexperienced.

Bob was with us for six weeks, and he was a delightful house guest. When he returned to Kenya, he left a thank-you note and a beautifully hand-painted picture of an African mother nursing her child, probably done by an African artist.

CHAPTER TWENTY-TWO
A Final Word

Writing this book has been a most enjoyable project for me. I have remembered, re-lived and recorded some of the saddest, scariest, funniest and most unusual happenings of my life in Kenya. I have seen how my experiences there have influenced the rest of my life and how the Lord brought things into my life to help me grow. Now at 93, as I look back over the years, I know I am one of His children. Several times His Spirit has spoken to my spirit to correct or warn or reassure me. I can see from all that has happened that I am important to Him – not because of what I can do for Him but because of His love for me and for all people He has created.

He placed me in a Christian home where, if possible, we were in church every Sunday. The sermons were far beyond my childish comprehension, but I understood at an early age Jesus had paid the penalty for my sins. At 11, I accepted Him as my Savior.

During my time in Kenya, I was privileged to watch as the Kipsigis tribe transitioned from a primitive tribe to a people taking their place in the civilized world. Changes were noticeable in clothing (from cowhides to fabrics) and in homes (from small, round, mud-and-wattle buildings to larger rectangular homes with several rooms, real windows and doors. Some homes were even made of cement blocks.)

By the time I came home in 1960, education for children had become the accepted standard, even for girls. Although the people were still using some of their traditional tribal "medicines" and treatments (some of them dangerous), they were open to learning things such as nutrition, sanitation and health care. The most gratifying changes to us as missionaries were the transformations in people when they became Christians.

About three-fourths of the way through writing this book, I was in the hospital and rehab for about 12 days. My daughter-in-law brought me a big box of letters I had written from Kenya. My mother had saved them all, but I had never taken the time to read them. While in rehab, I read all the letters from my first term (four-and-a-half years' worth). So when I came home, I had a couple of corrections to make.

A few things I had completely forgotten. For instance, during my first few months at Tenwek, we had frequent invasions of soldier ants in Freedom Hall. Our superintendent decided the ants had taken up enough of our time; so he told a couple of the workmen to find the nest and destroy it. The workmen followed a line of ants until the ants went into the ground, and then the workmen started digging. They dug a hole about three feet across and twelve to fifteen inches deep. When I looked into that hole, it was alive with ants. They were crawling on each other, and the mass appeared to be an inch or more thick. That ant nest was only twenty-five feet from our kitchen door. I don't remember how the workmen eradicated the ants, but they did. After that we rarely had an ant invasion.

I'm thankful for my years in Kenya and for the unique experiences I had there. And I'm thankful for the years in the United States. I'm especially thankful that the Lord allowed me to experience motherhood. Tricia and David and their spouses are all contributing, productive citizens who continue to make me proud and happy.

If you have been blessed by anything in the book, learned anything new, or just plain enjoyed it, please praise the Lord with me. I want God to get the credit. After all, He got me to Kenya in the first place. And He gave me the ability to remember clearly after 50 or 60 years the incidents that I have written about. He also, I now believe, brought me to Homewoods on the Willamette, which had an established Writer's Club with a well-qualified leader. When she learned that I had been a missionary, she encouraged me to write about some of my experiences. And after writing a few, I knew I wanted my grandchildren to know about some of the things. So, I kept writing and put the stories together into this book.

And finally, to my three grandchildren – and to all of you too:

1. Believe in Jesus. If you find believing hard, ask the Lord to give you faith, and He will do it because He does not want "anyone to perish, but everyone to come to repentance," II Peter 3:9.
2. Keep a diary or journal. Start storing up memories of things you would like to share someday with your grandchildren.
3. Go, give and pray. Get to know the missionaries from your church, help support them and pray for them. Go on a short-term mission trip if you have the chance. And if God should call you to full-time service, answer that call and embark on a great adventure with God.

May God bless you!

Millie Gackle at age 92

Made in the USA
Columbia, SC
04 April 2019